MAD
LOVE

Devan Rajkumar

MAD LOVE

Big Flavors Made to Share,
from South Asia to the West Indies

A COOKBOOK

Figure.1
Vancouver / Toronto / Berkeley

To my brother Jai, who inspired me to be better, take risks and follow my dreams. I trust we will break bread again in some way, shape or form.

Cataloguing data is available from Library and Archives Canada
ISBN 978-1-77327-232-0 (hbk.)

Design by Naomi MacDougall
Photography by Suech and Beck
Prop styling by Andrea McCrindle
Food styling by Melanie Stuparyk
Editing by Michelle Meade
Copy editing by Pam Robertson
Proofreading by Breanne MacDonald
Indexing by Iva Cheung
Photos on pages 4 and 8 were provided by the author.

Printed and bound in China by Shenzhen Reliance Printing Co., Ltd.
Distributed internationally by Publishers Group West

Figure 1 Publishing Inc.
Vancouver BC Canada
www.figure1publishing.com

Figure 1 Publishing is located in the traditional, unceded territory of the xʷməθkʷəy̓əm (Musqueam), Sḵwx̱wú7mesh (Squamish), and səlilwətaɬ (Tsleil-Waututh) peoples.

CONTENTS

INTRODUCTION

Oh man… *my own cookbook.*

In 2016 I was traveling the world, satiating my appetite for travel and culinary knowledge. I needed to explore and learn, despite the fact that I was a nearly broke (not broken) couch surfer and couldn't tell you where I was headed. Every day rewarded me with discoveries—beautiful, deep-rooted traditions and stories that went into every meal, the people behind those dishes, and the endless variety of flavorful ingredients from the world's terroir.

I always wanted to be a chef, but it was met with some resistance. In my culture and family, a traditional career path as a professional in a white-collar role promised financial security and career stability. I sensed disappointment from my father due to my pursuits to become a trained chef. He worried that the challenges of kitchen work and the grueling hours in a high-pressure environment might eventually take a physical (and mental) toll on me. I was determined to prove him wrong and make my parents proud.

For the longest time, my goal was to be an impeccable, top-rated chef with a flawless game and all the answers. I worked hard to become the executive chef for a national company and appeared on magazine covers and on television. My confidence was through the roof. I knew who I was and where I wanted to be; I thought I knew everything there was to know about food and cooking. It didn't help that I had surrounded myself with people who were gassing me up. Ask me anything, and I had an answer for you. Oh, did I have it all wrong.

I can't explain why I had such an ego. Maybe it was because of the endless hours laboring in the kitchen with late nights fueled by endorphins. Perhaps I was asserting a persona to overcompensate for a sense of guilt or validate my life decisions. I can't answer that. But I have learned that this age-old adage rings true: "Arrogance is the surest path to failure."

Early into my career, I had a calling to travel and explore the world. As I spent more time making discoveries in food, recipes and culture, the paradigm of my purpose shifted. The exposure to new foods and different ways of cooking left an impression—each country, region and, in some cases, city boasted unique ingredients. For instance, in India, the cuisine and ingredients changed every 100 km (62 miles). This was what you might call a rude awakening.

Those experiences and a journey of self-discovery led me to where I am today, in a constant state of curiosity. I am frequently humbled by how much exists in the food world and how much I have yet to learn and conquer. I no longer desired to be at the helm of a world-renowned restaurant; instead, I found greater purpose and joy in educating myself about the provenance of food and ingredients and sharing that knowledge with anyone interested.

I remain a student and forever keep a beginner's mindset. If you ask me today about my exciting food experiences, it's difficult to answer. My appreciation of a dish derives from its flavors, preparation and origins. These days, I spend more time asking questions, allowing curiosity about ingredients and people to guide my greatest career pursuits.

THE BACK STORY

I was born in Canada into a Guyanese household, and we frequented a local Hindu temple in the Greater Toronto Area (GTA). We were a close-knit family with an appreciation for our traditions and culture. We were heavily involved as active members of the broader West and East Indian community in the area. My grandmother "Ma," who lived with us, adored me and lovingly called me "Little Polkaroo." (A term of endearment inspired by

a mythical character on a children's TV show called *Polka Dot Door*.)

Although located in South America, Guyana is considered part of the Caribbean West Indies. When the British colonized India in the 19th century, Indians were transported across the Caribbean to become indentured servants. This history makes my story unique. While I am Guyanese, Caribbean and West Indian by heritage, I assimilate and feel at home in South Asian culture—after all, that's where my ancestry lies. This book proudly features everything from a classic Guyanese Pepperpot (page 127) to a Saffron Kheer (page 157), as I identify with both worlds.

I've advocated for my culture for decades, presenting our food traditions in the best light and elevating them. After spending countless years working with other culinary styles (French, Italian, Mexican, Japanese), my path took an extraordinary turn when I realized the importance of my culinary roots.

My mom is a phenomenal cook who would always test new recipes and take inspiration from her surroundings: things she saw on TV, through her travels or at someone else's home. (Remember, they were living without the internet back in the day.) She would then incorporate elements into the home-cooked meals she prepared for us. For example, we spent many evenings with my Uncle Joe and Aunty Maria. (They weren't biologically related to us, but they were like family and the terms are used as a form of respect—it's cultural.) The long table would be full of gloriously authentic Italian dishes. And it was here, as a kid, that I had my first Italian feast. We would start

with antipasti: fennel salad, olives, meats, cheeses and assorted finger foods. Then they'd roll out the dishes. Oh boy. The pasta. The meat. The dessert. My uncle cured salami, and I have vivid memories of him slicing it up for us kids. My brother and I were raised Hindu, and my mom would give the look of death when we reached for it and savored the flavors. Enjoying cured meats was an act of rebellion back then. Soon after, we began having finocchio (fennel) salad, eggplant Parmigiano-Reggiano and cheese boards at home.

As a child, I followed my mom around the kitchen. The aromatics, sights and sounds hypnotized me. Since I was so small, I would utilize a stool to give myself a better vantage point. And it helped me fulfil the requisite role of taster!

To this day, my mother continues to inspire me. My childhood in the kitchen and at the dining table have helped define my approach to cooking and recipe development. And the more I dig into Guyanese food and its history, the more I lean on my mother, who has become my greatest ally and supporter. My maternal grandmother passed away when I was ten years old, so when my mother passes down a recipe she learned from her mother, I feel an instant connection to my family's heritage, and it warms my heart. My grandmother would be so proud to see me sharing roti (page 56), okra (page 83) and dhal (page 79) recipes with the world.

← Some of my favorite shots from my travels.

HOW TO USE THIS BOOK

This book is a culmination of my decades-long relationship with food. Here, I share my favorite recipes and lessons from my travels, my people and my heritage. Expressions of my culinary journey include Hakka-Style Chili Chicken (page 112), Caribbean Ceviche (page 94) and Keema Parathas (page 64). Others, including Palak Paneer Spanakopita (page 74) and Caribbean Risotto with Crispy Salmon (page 96), are inspired by the best of my culinary escapades across the globe. One thing they have in common? They're all simple, delicious and loaded with glorious flavor.

I have included a few gluten-free and/or vegan versions of classic West and East Indian dishes, given my viewers' frequent requests for them. And when it comes to dietary requirements, each recipe features icons to help readers quickly identify the best-suited recipes. The symbols are:

 VEGETARIAN   DAIRY-FREE

 VEGAN   NUT-FREE

 GLUTEN-FREE   30 MINUTES OR LESS

RECIPE NOTES
Unless otherwise specified:
Black pepper is freshly ground.
Eggs are large.
Flour is all-purpose.
Herbs are always fresh.
Parsley is flat leaf (Italian).
Salt is kosher.
Vegetables are medium-sized.

I hope to empower you to cook for your friends and family and inspire you to expand your palate by traveling the world. It can be daunting to step out of your comfort zone, but these recipes will encourage you to introduce different cultures to the plate. And I urge you to be forever humble, open-minded and curious—learn to fall in love with being a student.

These recipes serve as a foundation for your repertoire. Once you grow more confident and efficient in the kitchen, try to adapt my versions and make them your own. Switch things up with local or seasonal ingredients, your favorite pantry staples or leftovers in the fridge. And remember to share your inventions! It fills me with pride when my viewers and readers tell me how they've adapted my recipes or applied some of my techniques when they cook.

The recipes in this book should inspire you to get into the kitchen and start cooking. Don't feel handcuffed to them—they are here to serve you, to provide a framework for you to become more confident in the kitchen. No Thai chili peppers? Replace them with habaneros. Out of maple syrup? Try honey instead. I encourage using local ingredients and items you already stock in the pantry. Take the energy and essence from these recipes to breathe life and inspiration into your cooking. What's the meaning of the title, you might wonder. Many of my viewers will recognize this trademark sign-off from my videos. I have so much gratitude for everything: my career, my friends and family, my audience. It's the ultimate expression to sum up everything I feel when I explore a new part of the world, discover a new ingredient, and champion my culture and heritage. It's also what the world needs right now. But you probably know that.

So, enough said. We're here to have some fun. Now let's learn together and start cooking with mad flavor and mad love.

CHEF DEVAN'S "EAST × WEST" PANTRY ESSENTIALS

While these ingredients may seem unusual, they're an integral part of my cooking and bring maximum flavor to dishes. Best of all, these days most are easy to find at larger supermarkets or online.

AMCHUR POWDER Known as *amchoor* or dried mango powder, this fruity spice is made from dried unripe mangoes and used to enhance curries, pickles, soups, chutneys, fruit salads and more.

CASSAVA Native to South America, cassava (or yuca) is a starchy tuber, like a yam or sweet potato. It can be mashed, made into breads and chips, or added to soups and stews. See more on page 85.

CASSAREEP See page 128.

CHAAT MASALA This aromatic South Asian spice blend is typically made with cumin, coriander, amchoor powder, ground ginger, asafetida, chili powder, black salt and black pepper. Use it to add tanginess to salads or vinaigrettes (page 44).

CHILI PEPPERS Chili peppers feature in many of my recipes. Depending on the application, they can add heat, sweetness and even smokiness to enliven the simplest dishes. I commonly use Wiri Wiri peppers—small, round chilis from Guyana—but I also like Thai bird's eye chilis. Wiri Wiri peppers can be substituted with half the amount of Scotch bonnet or habanero chilis.

CULANTRO (*CHADON BENI*) This fragrant herb with broad, sturdy leaves is also called Mexican coriander, sawtooth coriander or *chadon beni*. It tastes like a sharp, peppery cilantro, and I like the freshness it brings to dishes like Pineapple Chow (page 43).

CURRY LEAVES The fragrant leaves bring a distinct flavor—earthy, nutty and smoky, all at once—to soups and curries, including the Keralan Fish Curry (page 104). When possible, use fresh curry leaves, which have a more intense flavor.

CURRY POWDERS Curry powders add depths of flavor to curries and stews. Guyanese curry powder is made up of a fragrant blend of coriander, turmeric, cumin, black pepper, fenugreek, mustard seeds and cardamom. I also use a spicy curry powder called Madras curry powder. In a pinch, you can substitute a regular curry powder for either.

DRIED ORANGE PEEL I don't use this ingredient often, but it is essential for the classic Pepperpot on page 127 (or see page 77 for the vegan version). The natural oils add a beautiful fragrance to the dish.

FENUGREEK LEAVES, DRIED (*KASOORI METHI*) The unusual bitterness of this dried herb adds heaps of flavor (some say celery and maple) to soups, sauces, vegetables and curries.

GARAM MASALA This aromatic spice blend brings flavor and warmth to dishes. It combines cloves, cinnamon, cardamom, cumin, coriander, nutmeg, bay, mace and black pepper. This is essential in my spice rack, and I use it generously in the Guyanese Chicken Curry (page 116).

GHEE Its name originating from the Sanskrit word for "sprinkled," ghee is clarified butter. To make it, butter is heated low and slow and then strained to remove the milk solids. It is then cooked longer until golden, nutty and fragrant.

KASHMIRI CHILI POWDER This beautiful spice is designed to add more color (rather than heat) to dishes and features across many of the recipes in this book, including Masala Mac 'n' Cheese with Butternut Squash (page 21) and Keema Parathas (page 64).

RED CHILI POWDER An integral part of desi cuisine, and also known as *lal mirch*. Adds a beautiful red color when used and a distinct taste and aroma. Made from ground red chili peppers with the seeds still inside.

TAMARIND SAUCE Made from puréed tamarind that has been boiled then seasoned with sugar and other spices. It is sweet, sour, tart and one of my favorite ingredients to cook with. Used widely in Southeast Asian dishes. It adds so much flavor and can balance out the sweetness in curries, and even Shrimp Pad Thai (page 31).

TANDOORI MASALA Tandoori masala is an Indian spice blend used to enhance grilled meats traditionally cooked in a tandoor, or clay oven. Its distinctive red color sets it apart from other blends. Tandoori masala is most often used to coat meats, but I also add it to the basting butter in my Tandoori Steak with Chimichurri (page 124).

PUMP UP

My brother Jai fueled my love for music, which is now an integral aspect of my cooking—from prep to service. Here are some of my favorite playlists: songs on heavy rotation, melodies from my childhood and tunes from travels around the world.

I love the power of music. Like food, it can energize you, stimulate your senses and transport you to another time and place.

Rap City

RESPIRATION
Black Star (featuring Common)

THE SCORE
Fugees (featuring Diamond D)

PROTECT YA NECK
Wu-Tang Clan

BROWN MUNDE
AP Dhillon

POUND CAKE
Drake (featuring Jay-Z)

IT AIN'T HARD TO TELL
Nas

93 'TIL INFINITY
Souls of Mischief

ELECTRIC RELAXATION
A Tribe Called Quest

FULL CLIP
Gang Starr

MY WORLD
O.C.

SIDHU SON
Sidhu Moose Wala

LIVIN' PROOF
Group Home

FAMILY BUSINESS
Fugees

LUCHINI
Camp Lo

MATHEMATICS
Mos Def

DEFINITION
Black Star

QUIET STORM
Mobb Deep

REAL HIP-HOP
Das EFX

DANGER
Blahzay Blahzay

ATLIENS
Outkast

PICTURE ME ROLLIN'
2Pac

COME CLEAN
Jeru the Damaja

THE SEED (2.0)
The Roots (featuring Cody Chesnutt)

1NCE AGAIN
A Tribe Called Quest

Island Vibes

WHAT HAPPENS IN DE PARTY
Rupee

HELLO
Kes

FALUMA
Alison Hinds

PUMP ME UP
Krosfyah (featuring Edwin Yearwood)

WOTLESS
Kes

BACCHANALIST
Kerwin Du Bois

OVER AND OVER AGAIN
Tami Chynn

LOST ONES
Lauryn Hill

JUMP
Rupee

TO YOUR ARMS WITH LOVE
Jah Cure

ROAD TO ZION
Damian Marley (featuring Nas)

WEST INDIES
Koffee

STATION PE GADI
Babla and Kanchan

IT'S CARNIVAL
Destra (featuring Machel Montano)

TEASE ME
Chaka Demus and Pliers

HERE I AM BABY
UB40

BOLO BOLO
Babla and Kanchan

DULAHIN CHALE SASURAL
Rakesh Yankaran

BLIND TO YOU
Collie Buddz

GYAL YOU A PARTY ANIMAL
Charly Black

DRY CRY
Sizzla

THE JAM

The '80s Throwback

WALKING ON BROKEN GLASS
Annie Lennox

COME UNDONE
Duran Duran

THE SWEETEST TABOO
Sade

JOLENE
Dolly Parton

OUT OF TOUCH
Hall and Oates

LOVE IS A BATTLEFIELD
Pat Benatar

TAKE ON ME
a-ha

EVERYWHERE
Fleetwood Mac

EASY LOVER
Phil Collins and Philip Bailey

YOUR LOVE
The Outfield

LA ISLA BONITA
Madonna

THE LONGEST TIME
Billy Joel

EROTIC CITY
Prince

LITTLE LIES
Fleetwood Mac

LET'S DANCE
David Bowie

EVERYTHING SHE WANTS
Wham!

This One Goes to Eleven

UNTIL THE END
OF THE WORLD
U2

THERE THERE
Radiohead

JEREMY
Pearl Jam

ROUND HERE
Counting Crows

BANQUET
Bloc Party

LET DOWN
Radiohead

THE LESS I KNOW
THE BETTER
Tame Impala

DAY TRIPPER
The Beatles

HELP I'M ALIVE
Metric

DIAMONDS ON THE
SOLES OF HER SHOES
Paul Simon

CALIFORNIA DREAMIN'
The Mamas & The Papas

15 STEP
Radiohead

SULTANS OF SWING
Dire Straits

INTERSTATE LOVE SONG
Stone Temple Pilots

GOOD FOOD, GOOD FRIENDS

SHARED PLATES

FRIED PLANTAINS

SERVES 4

2 ripe plantains, peeled
and ends trimmed

2 Tbsp coconut oil,
plus extra if needed

When I was a kid, the inviting scent of sweet plantains caramelizing in a pan would compel me to jump out of bed in the mornings and race down the stairs so fast my feet barely touched the ground. I would devour them as soon as they were made—often, I'd scald the roof of my mouth in the process. I couldn't help myself: the temptation was always too irresistible—especially when Mom coated them with cinnamon and maple syrup.

Enjoy these fried plantains as a snack or as a side at any meal.

Line a baking sheet with parchment paper.

Cut plantains diagonally into ¼-inch-thick slices.

Heat oil in a cast-iron skillet over medium heat and brush evenly across pan. Add plantains in batches and sear for 3–4 minutes per side, until golden brown. Transfer to the prepared baking sheet. Repeat with the remaining plantains, adding more oil if necessary.

VARIATION

FRIED PLANTAINS WITH CINNAMON AND MAPLE SYRUP

2 Tbsp maple syrup

⅓ tsp ground cinnamon

⅓ tsp ground allspice

¼ tsp ground nutmeg

FRIED PLANTAINS WITH CINNAMON AND MAPLE SYRUP In a small bowl, combine all ingredients. Brush both sides of the fried plantains with the mixture and serve.

MASALA MAC 'N' CHEESE
WITH BUTTERNUT SQUASH

SERVES 4–6

BUTTERNUT SQUASH
1 butternut squash, peeled, seeded and cut into bite-sized pieces
Sprig of rosemary
Salt and white pepper, to taste
1 Tbsp olive oil

MAC 'N' CHEESE
3 cups dry short-cut pasta
2½ cups 2% milk
3 Tbsp butter, plus extra for greasing
1 Tbsp Ginger-Garlic Paste (page 167)
1 tsp Kashmiri chili powder
½ tsp ground cumin
½ tsp ground coriander
½ tsp ground turmeric
½ tsp dried fenugreek leaves (*kasoori methi*)
3 Tbsp flour
Pinch of ground nutmeg
Salt and white pepper, to taste
1 clove garlic, finely chopped
2 cups grated cheddar
¼ cup grated Parmigiano-Reggiano
¼ cup grated Asiago cheese
1 tsp Dijon mustard
1 tsp store-bought or homemade Hot Sauce (page 140) (optional)

ASSEMBLY
¾ cup grated mozzarella
½ cup panko breadcrumbs
2 Tbsp finely chopped chives, for garnish

Few dishes in life bring me as much comfort and joy as a classic mac 'n' cheese. Boosted with a medley of cheeses, sweet squash and my favorite spices, this tasty reinvention (also a midweek staple in my home) is extra. You know what I'm talking about: the type of comfort food that is best shared with others. Plus, it's a great way to sneak in the veg for the kids. Tasting is believing.

BUTTERNUT SQUASH Preheat oven to 400°F. Line a baking sheet with parchment paper.

In a bowl, combine all ingredients and toss well. Transfer to the prepared baking sheet and bake for 20 minutes. Discard rosemary and set squash aside. (Leave the oven on for baking the mac 'n' cheese.)

MAC 'N' CHEESE Meanwhile, bring a large saucepan of salted water to a boil. Add dry pasta and cook according to package instructions. Drain, then set aside.

Bring milk to a simmer in a saucepan. Grease a large baking dish.

Melt butter in a separate large saucepan over medium-low heat. Add ginger-garlic paste, chili powder, cumin, coriander, turmeric and fenugreek leaves. Mix well. Add flour and stir for 2–3 minutes, until it begins to smell nutty. Gradually whisk in milk, ensuring there are no lumps.

Increase heat to medium and whisk for 2–3 minutes, until thickened. Remove from heat, then season with nutmeg, salt and pepper.

Fold in garlic, cheddar, Parmigiano-Reggiano, Asiago, Dijon and hot sauce (if using). Using an immersion blender, blend until smooth.

ASSEMBLY Gently fold pasta, mozzarella and butternut squash into the sauce. Transfer mixture to the prepared baking dish. Top with an even layer of panko breadcrumbs. Bake for 15 minutes, until the cheese sauce is bubbling around the edges, then remove from oven. Set broiler to high, then return the dish to the oven and broil until golden brown on top, approximately 1–2 minutes.

Garnish with chives and serve warm.

DESI CAULIFLOWER NACHOS

SERVES 4

CAULIFLOWER

1 head cauliflower, cut into florets

2–3 Tbsp grapeseed oil

1 tsp smoked paprika

1 tsp garlic powder

1 tsp onion powder

1 tsp garam masala

1 tsp amchur powder

1 tsp black salt

1 tsp red chili powder

CHIVE SOUR CREAM

1 cup sour cream

¼ cup thinly sliced chives

½ tsp salt

½ tsp black pepper

2 tsp lemon juice

1 tsp lemon zest

ASSEMBLY

2 cups grated cheddar

1 avocado, pitted and finely chopped

1 Roma tomato, diced

1 mango, cut into thin strips

2–3 Thai green chili peppers, to taste, thinly sliced

Chopped cilantro, for garnish

Green Chutney (page 176), Tamarind-Date Chutney (page 176) and Smoked Raita (page 177), to serve

Cauliflower makes a welcome alternative to classic tortilla chip–based nachos. Here, I've seasoned it with aromatic spices, then baked it until golden. It's cooked long enough to have some tenderness, but it retains some much-needed crunch for textural interest. No doubt about it, this accessible crowd-pleaser rewards with every delicious bite.

CAULIFLOWER Preheat oven to 450°F. Line a baking sheet with aluminum foil.

Place cauliflower in a bowl and drizzle evenly with oil. Add remaining ingredients and mix well. Transfer cauliflower to the prepared baking sheet. Bake for 8–10 minutes, until golden brown but still crunchy.

CHIVE SOUR CREAM Combine all ingredients in a bowl and mix well.

ASSEMBLY Remove the cauliflower from the oven. Change the oven setting to broil.

Sprinkle cheddar over cauliflower, then return the baking sheet to the oven and broil for 3–4 minutes, until melted. Keep an eye on the pan to prevent it from burning.

Transfer the cauliflower to a serving platter. Top with avocado, tomato, mango, chili peppers, cilantro and chive sour cream.

Serve immediately with green chutney, tamarind-date chutney and smoked raita—and prepare to feast!

GUYANESE EGG BALLS

MAKES 6

EGG BALLS

6 eggs

1 lb cassava or potatoes, peeled and cut into ½-inch cubes (see page 85)

1¾ tsp salt (divided)

2 scallions, thinly sliced

2 Wiri Wiri chili peppers, finely chopped (see Note)

1 tsp onion powder

1 tsp garlic powder

¾ tsp ground cumin

½ tsp black pepper

Grapeseed oil, for greasing

COATING

1 cup flour

2 eggs, beaten

1 cup panko breadcrumbs, gently pulsed

Salt and black pepper, to taste

ASSEMBLY

Vegetable or grapeseed oil, for deep-frying

Tamarind-Date Chutney (page 176), Mango Sour (page 175) and/or store-bought or homemade Hot Sauce (page 140), to serve

I suspect this tasty snack could be a distant cousin of the British Scotch egg or the Nigerian egg roll (or maybe a marriage of the two). A boiled egg is wrapped in cassava mash and then deep-fried until golden. I like to coat the egg balls in fine panko breadcrumbs, which are drier and flakier than regular breadcrumbs, so the coating is light and crunchy.

EGG BALLS Bring a saucepan of water to a boil. Gently lower eggs and boil for 6–8 minutes, depending on your desired firmness of the yolk. Transfer the eggs to a bowl of ice water to stop them from cooking. When cool enough to handle, peel eggs and set aside.

Bring another saucepan of water to a boil. Add cassava (or potato) and 1 tsp salt and boil for 15–20 minutes, until fork tender. Drain, then transfer to a large bowl and mash until smooth. Stir in scallions, Wiri Wiri chili peppers, onion powder, garlic powder, cumin, the remaining ¾ tsp salt and pepper.

Rub a little oil on your hands to prevent sticking. Place a ½ cup of filling into the palm of your hand and flatten it out to form an oval shape, about ⅓ inch thick. Place an egg in the middle and gently press the filling around the egg. Repeat for the remaining eggs.

COATING Place flour, beaten eggs and panko into three separate shallow bowls. Season each with salt and pepper.

ASSEMBLY Heat oil in a deep fryer or a large saucepan, a third full, over medium-high heat, until it reaches a temperature of 350°F. Line a baking sheet with paper towels.

Roll an egg ball in the flour, then shake off excess. Dip into beaten egg, then press firmly with panko. Repeat with remaining egg balls.

Carefully lower egg balls into the fryer or saucepan, taking care not to splash hot oil. Deep-fry for 2–3 minutes, until golden brown all over. Using a slotted spoon, transfer the egg balls to the prepared baking sheet to drain.

Serve immediately with chutney, mango sour and/or hot sauce.

> NOTE: Wiri Wiri chili peppers can be substituted with half the amount of Scotch bonnet or habanero chili peppers.

GUYANESE CHEESE ROLLS

MAKES 9

DOUGH

2½ cups flour, plus extra for dusting

⅔ cup (1⅓ sticks) frozen butter, grated

1 tsp curry powder

1 tsp salt

CHEESE FILLING

2 scallions, thinly sliced

1½ cups grated sharp cheddar

½ cup black truffle pecorino (see Note)

1 tsp dried fenugreek leaves (*kasoori methi*)

1 tsp thyme leaves

¾ tsp onion powder

¾ tsp garlic powder

½ tsp paprika

1–2 Tbsp store-bought or homemade Hot Sauce (page 140), to taste

2 tsp Dijon mustard

Salt and black pepper, to taste

ASSEMBLY

1 egg, beaten, for brushing

This delicious snack is sold at snackettes and markets all across Guyana. As a child, I'd come home from school and immediately recognize the smell of freshly baked cheese rolls. I'd grab a roll (okay, maybe two) and douse them with extra pepper sauce (obvs). Here is my take on tradition.

DOUGH In a large bowl, combine flour, butter, curry powder and salt. Using your hands, slowly incorporate the butter throughout the flour, until it forms pea-sized lumps.

Pour in ¾ cup ice-cold water and mix to form a soft, pliable dough. Wrap in plastic wrap and refrigerate for at least 30 minutes.

CHEESE FILLING In a large bowl, combine all ingredients. Mix well.

ASSEMBLY Preheat oven to 375°F. Line a baking sheet with parchment paper.

Cut dough into 9 pieces. On a lightly floured surface, roll a piece of dough into a 6 × 8-inch rectangle, about ⅛ inch thick. Brush edges with egg wash. Add 2 Tbsp of cheese filling along one long side of the rectangle and fold over dough once. Add 2 Tbsp of cheese filling and fold over a second time. Fold over a third and final time to close the cheese roll, seam side facing down. Use your fingers to pinch the seam back into the dough to seal it shut. Using a fork, crimp along the edges to secure the filling. Repeat with the remaining dough pieces and cheese filling.

Place rolls on the prepared baking sheet, then brush with egg wash. Bake for 20 minutes, until lightly browned.

NOTE: Truffle pecorino, or *pecorino al tartufo*, is an Italian sheep's milk cheese infused with black truffles. Buttery and nutty, a little goes a long way when you want the truffle aroma. You can find it at specialty delis and cheesemongers.

TRINIDADIAN DOUBLES

SERVES 4–6

FLATBREAD (*BARA*)

1 tsp active dried yeast

1½ tsp sugar

2 cups flour, plus extra for dusting

¾ tsp baking powder

½ tsp ground turmeric

½ tsp salt

Vegetable oil, for greasing and frying

CURRIED CHICKPEA FILLING (*CHANNA*)

2 Tbsp vegetable oil

1 small onion, finely chopped

3 cloves garlic, finely chopped

1 (19-oz) can chickpeas, drained and rinsed

2 Tbsp Green Seasoning (page 167)

1 tsp curry powder

1 tsp garam masala

½ tsp cumin

1 tsp amchur powder

½ Scotch bonnet chili pepper, finely chopped

Salt and black pepper, to taste

CUCUMBER CHUTNEY

2 cups peeled and grated cucumber

1 clove garlic, finely chopped

1 Tbsp Green Seasoning (page 167)

½ tsp salt

1 tsp fresh lime juice

ASSEMBLY

1 cup vegetable oil, plus extra for greasing

Tamarind-Date Chutney (page 176)

Store-bought or homemade Hot Sauce (page 140) and/or Mango Sour (page 175)

*Rob Base and E-Z Rock said it best: it takes two to make a thing go right. While doubles have a ubiquitous presence throughout the Caribbean—especially in Trinidad and Tobago—this snack originated in India. Two fried pieces of dough (*bara*) sandwich a spiced chickpea curry known as* channa. *Finish it with lashings of hot sauces and there you have it, my friends—my all-time favorite vegan dish.*

FLATBREAD (*BARA*) In a large bowl, combine yeast and sugar. Pour in ¾ cup + 3 Tbsp warm water. Set aside for 5 minutes, until bubbles start to form.

Add flour, baking powder, turmeric and salt and mix well. Using your hands, knead dough until a ball is formed. (Alternatively, prepare the dough in a stand mixer with the dough hook attachment.)

Oil a large bowl, then add dough. Cover with a dish towel and set aside for 1–2 hours, or until doubled in size.

CURRIED CHICKPEA FILLING (*CHANNA*) Meanwhile, heat oil in a frying pan over medium heat. Add onion and garlic and sauté for 7 minutes, until onion is softened and translucent. Reduce heat, if necessary, to avoid burning.

Stir in chickpeas, spices and chili pepper. Season to taste with salt and black pepper. Sauté for 4–5 minutes until flavors mingle. Pour in 2 cups water and bring to a gentle boil. Reduce heat to medium-low, partially cover and simmer for 35–40 minutes. Using the back of a spoon, mash some of the chickpeas to thicken filling.

CUCUMBER CHUTNEY Combine all ingredients in a bowl and mix well. Refrigerate until needed.

ASSEMBLY Heat oil in a cast-iron frying pan over medium-high heat until it reaches a temperature of 350°F.

Lightly oil a clean work surface. Take a small piece of dough (slightly smaller than a golf ball) and cover unused dough with a dish towel. Using your hands, press out into a thin disk, about 4–5 inches in diameter. Repeat with the remaining dough balls.

Working in batches to avoid overcrowding, carefully lower the flatbreads into the hot oil and fry for 3–4 seconds on each side, until golden. Transfer to a paper towel–lined plate to drain excess oil. Repeat with remaining flatbreads. Makes about 14–16 pieces.

Place 2 flatbreads, side by side and slightly overlapping, on each plate. Top both pieces with 3 Tbsp of curried chickpea filling, 1 Tbsp cucumber chutney, 1–2 tsp tamarind-date chutney and hot sauce (and/or mango sour). Serve warm.

GUYANESE PHOLOURIE

MAKES 20

¾ tsp active dry yeast

½ cup yellow split peas, soaked in hot water for at least 1 hour

4 cloves garlic

2 Wiri Wiri chili peppers, thinly sliced (see Note)

1 cup flour

¾ tsp curry powder

1 tsp baking powder

½ tsp ground cumin

¼ tsp red chili powder

1 tsp salt

2 scallions, thinly sliced

2 cups vegetable oil, for frying

Mango Sour (page 175) and/or Tamarind-Date Chutney (page 176), to serve

Some of my fondest food memories come from Guyana, where we would travel to on family holidays when I was a child. This delicious snack is one of those dishes.

Split peas, all-purpose flour and aromatic spices join forces to create a thick batter, which is fried to perfection. They're super more-ish, especially when they're served up with chutney—it seems almost impossible (and unfair) to eat just one.

In a small bowl, combine yeast and ½ cup warm water. Set aside for 5 minutes, or until foamy.

Drain split peas. In a blender or food processor, combine split peas, garlic and Wiri Wiri chili peppers and blend until smooth.

In a large bowl, combine flour, curry powder, baking powder, cumin, chili powder and salt. Pour in the split pea mixture from the blender. Stir in the yeast mixture, then fold in scallions and combine well. Cover with a dish towel and set aside to rest for an hour.

Heat oil in a large saucepan over medium-high heat, until it reaches a temperature of 350°F. Carefully lower small balls of the batter (about 1 tsp each) into the fryer, taking care not to splash hot oil. Deep-fry for 2–3 minutes, until golden brown. Transfer to a paper towel–lined plate to drain excess oil. Serve with mango sour and/or tamarind-date chutney.

NOTE: Wiri Wiri chili peppers can be substituted with half the amount of Scotch bonnet or habanero chili peppers.

SHRIMP PAD THAI

SERVES 2

SAUCE
2 Tbsp fish sauce
2 Tbsp oyster sauce
1½ Tbsp tamarind sauce
1 Tbsp rice wine vinegar
1 Tbsp soy sauce
1 Tbsp brown sugar

PAD THAI
4 tsp sesame oil (divided)
1 lb large (16/20) shrimp,
peeled and deveined
¾ cup diced firm tofu
3–5 Thai red or green chili peppers,
thinly sliced
1 carrot, thinly sliced into rounds
1 red bell pepper, seeded,
deveined and thinly sliced
½ onion, sliced
1 cup small broccoli florets
1 cup thinly sliced shiitake mushrooms
Salt and black pepper, to taste
8 oz rice noodles, soaked in warm water
for 10 minutes and drained
2 eggs, beaten
2 scallions, chopped

GARNISH
Bean sprouts
Cilantro leaves
Lime wedges
½ cup chopped peanuts, toasted

When we were teenagers, my brother Jai introduced me to pad Thai at the Toronto restaurant Salad King. While the restaurant has since expanded, I will always cherish its former iteration—a hidden gem with only two tables (literally) where Jai and I frequently dined. These days, whenever I eat Thai food, I am reminded of the laughs we shared.

SAUCE In a bowl, combine all ingredients and mix well. Set aside.

PAD THAI Heat 2 tsp oil in a wok or large frying pan over high heat. Add shrimp and sauté for 1–2 minutes, until shrimp is slightly opaque. Transfer to a plate and set aside.

In the same pan, heat the remaining 2 tsp oil over medium-high heat. Add tofu and sauté for 1–2 minutes, until golden brown. Transfer to a plate and set aside.

To the same pan, add chili peppers, carrot, bell pepper, onion, broccoli and mushrooms. Season with salt and black pepper. Sauté for 1–2 minutes. Reduce heat to medium.

Stir in noodles and ¼ cup sauce. Push the noodles and sauce to one side of the pan and pour beaten eggs into the center. Cook for 30–45 seconds, until just scrambled, and gently fold into the noodles. Stir in shrimp, tofu and scallions. Season to taste with salt and black pepper.

Transfer to a serving platter. Garnish with bean sprouts, cilantro, lime wedges and peanuts.

GUYANESE-STYLE CHICKEN CHOW MEIN

SERVES 4

MARINATED CHICKEN

2 lbs bone-in chicken thighs

2 Tbsp Green Seasoning (page 167)

1 Tbsp Ginger-Garlic Paste (page 167)

2 tsp vegetable oil, plus extra for greasing

1 Tbsp soy sauce

2 tsp cassareep

1 tsp salt

¾ tsp ground cumin

¾ tsp ground coriander

1 Wiri Wiri chili pepper, finely chopped (see Note)

1 tsp five-spice powder

1 tsp thyme leaves

CHOW MEIN

12 oz uncooked chow mein

4 tsp sesame oil (divided)

1 Tbsp soy sauce

1 tsp salt (divided)

1 red bell pepper, seeded, deveined and sliced

1 carrot, grated

½ white onion, sliced

¾ cup long beans, cut into 2-inch segments (see Note)

¾ cup shredded cabbage

2 Tbsp Ginger-Garlic Paste (page 167)

2 scallions, chopped

2–3 Wiri Wiri chili peppers, to taste, thinly sliced (see Note)

¾ tsp black pepper

Who makes the best chow mein? My grandmother. But this just happens to be the next best thing.

No Guyanese gathering is complete without a chow mein of sorts, a popular dish introduced by Chinese immigrants. (Fun fact: we spell it as one word in Guyana, as in chow-mein.) I've provided a classic recipe, but this dish is super versatile so feel free to play with the flavors. You can pack it with proteins, toss in colorful veg or spice it up with your favorite seasonings. So good.

MARINATED CHICKEN Using a paring knife, make several slices along the chicken thighs, to the bone, to allow marinade to penetrate. Transfer chicken thighs to a bowl, add remaining ingredients and mix well, then cover and refrigerate. Allow to marinate for at least 2 hours but preferably overnight for best results.

Remove the chicken from the fridge and set aside for 30 minutes. Preheat the BBQ to medium heat. Oil the grates.

Add chicken to the grill, discarding the marinade. Grill for 20–25 minutes, turning occasionally, until evenly browned and the internal temperature reaches 165°F. Transfer to a plate and set aside.

CHOW MEIN Bring a large saucepan of salted water to a boil. Add chow mein and cook for 5 minutes, until tender. Drain, then transfer to a mixing bowl. Add 2 tsp sesame oil, soy sauce and ½ tsp salt.

Heat the remaining 2 tsp sesame oil in a large wok or large frying pan over high heat. Add bell pepper, carrot, onion, beans and cabbage. Stir in ginger-garlic paste, scallions, Wiri Wiri chili peppers, the remaining ½ tsp salt and black pepper. Sauté for 2–3 minutes, tossing frequently. Reduce heat to low and stir in the chow mein.

Transfer to a serving plate, top with chicken and serve immediately.

> NOTE: Long beans, also known as bora beans, snake beans or Chinese long beans, have a distinct and pronounced bean taste. They're often steamed, stir-fried or braised. Purchase them at Asian supermarkets or substitute them with green beans.
>
> Wiri Wiri chili peppers can be substituted with half the amount of Scotch bonnet or habanero chili peppers.

SMASHED ALOO TIKKI

SERVES 6

SMASHED POTATOES

2–3 Tbsp grapeseed oil

2 lbs baby red potatoes, unpeeled

½ tsp Kashmiri chili powder

¾ tsp garlic powder

¾ tsp onion powder

¾ tsp ground coriander

¾ tsp amchur powder

¾ tsp black salt

½ tsp ground cumin

Salt and black pepper, to taste

ASSEMBLY

½ stalk celery, finely chopped

¼ cup grated Parmigiano-Reggiano

2 Tbsp finely chopped cilantro

2–3 Thai green chili peppers, thinly sliced

1 Tbsp lemon zest

Pomegranate seeds, for garnish (optional)

Green Chutney (page 176), Tamarind-Date Chutney (page 176) and/or Smoked Raita (page 177), to serve

Aloo tikki are savory fried patties made of mashed potatoes mixed with herbs and spices, and are a popular chaat dish often sold by street vendors. This take is inspired by everyone's favorite spud variation: smashed potatoes! As with the traditional snack, the key to this delicious aloo tikki is a crispy, spicy crust.

SMASHED POTATOES Preheat oven to 425°F. Drizzle oil on a baking sheet.

Place potatoes in a large saucepan with cold water. Bring to a boil and simmer for 12–15 minutes, until fork tender. Drain.

Using your hands or the base of a glass, smash the potatoes but keep them in one piece. (Alternatively, you can use a 2-inch ring mold for a more uniform shape.) Place on the prepared baking sheet and turn to coat both sides with oil. In a bowl, combine chili powder, garlic powder, onion powder, coriander, amchur powder, black salt, cumin, salt and pepper. Sprinkle the potatoes with the spice blend and roast for 10–15 minutes, until golden and crispy. Flip and roast for 5 minutes longer, until both sides are crispy.

ASSEMBLY Arrange smashed potatoes on a serving platter and garnish with celery, Parmigiano-Reggiano, cilantro, chili peppers and pomegranate seeds (if using), and sprinkle with lemon zest. Serve warm with green chutney, tamarind-date chutney and/or smoked raita.

POUTINE EH!

SERVES 4

GRAVY
2 tsp grapeseed oil

1 large onion, chopped (1 cup)

1 tsp salt

½ tsp black pepper

4 cloves garlic

1 cup chopped portobello mushrooms

1 cup chopped cremini mushrooms

1 cup chopped shiitake mushrooms

3 sprigs thyme

Sprig of rosemary

2 Tbsp balsamic vinegar

2 tsp soy sauce

1 tsp brown sugar

1 tsp cornstarch

POUTINE
Vegetable oil, for frying

4 cups frozen French fries

Salt

1 cup cheese curds

Chopped chives, for garnish

C'mon, how could I NOT add this recipe?! Our national dish ticks all the comfort food boxes: something starchy (potatoes, check), something salty (cheese curds, check) and all of it smothered in a rich, indulgent gravy (check, check, check). Apart from denim-on-denim (#Canadiantuxedo), nothing gets more Canadian than this.

GRAVY Heat oil in a saucepan over medium heat. Add onion, salt and pepper and sauté for 7–8 minutes, until golden brown. Add garlic and sauté for another minute, until fragrant. Stir in mushrooms, thyme and rosemary and sauté for 7–8 minutes.

Add vinegar, soy sauce and brown sugar and mix well. Pour in 1½ cups water and simmer for 10 minutes. Mix cornstarch with 1–2 Tbsp water and add to the pan, then simmer for 5 minutes, until thickened. Remove rosemary and thyme sprigs.

Using an immersion blender, blend gravy until smooth. Set aside.

POUTINE Heat oil in a deep fryer or a large saucepan, a third full, over medium-high heat, until it reaches a temperature of 350°F. Carefully lower fries into the pan, taking care not to splash hot oil. Deep-fry for 6–7 minutes, until golden brown. Transfer to a paper towel–lined plate to drain excess oil. Season with salt.

Transfer fries to a serving plate. Top with cheese curds and ladle with gravy. Garnish with chives and serve.

PEPPERPOT TACOS

WITH RED CABBAGE SLAW AND WIRI WIRI MAYO

SERVES 4

PEPPERPOT TACOS
2 cups Pepperpot (page 127)

RED CABBAGE SLAW
3 scallions, thinly sliced
2 cups thinly sliced red cabbage
¼ cup Wiri Wiri Mayo (page 52)
¾ tsp salt
1 Tbsp fresh lemon juice

ASSEMBLY
1 small white onion, finely chopped
½ cup cilantro, finely chopped
8 small soft corn tortillas or
hard taco shells
1 lime, sliced into wedges, to serve

PEPPERPOT TACOS In a small saucepan, heat pepperpot and bring to a simmer over medium-low heat. Transfer to a dish and remove any bones and pull meat. Add back to pot and keep warm for serving.

RED CABBAGE SLAW In a large bowl, combine all ingredients and mix well.

ASSEMBLY In a small bowl, combine onion and cilantro.

If using soft tortillas, gently warm in a frying pan over medium heat for 30–45 seconds. Transfer to a plate and cover with a dish towel to keep warm.

To assemble tacos, spoon pepperpot into each tortilla or taco shell. Top with coleslaw and onion-cilantro salad. Serve with lime wedges.

THE
WEEKEND

BRUNCH

GRILLED BROCCOLINI CHAAT

SERVES 4–6

1 bunch broccolini
1½ Tbsp grapeseed oil
1 tsp salt
¾ tsp freshly cracked black pepper
½ cup Citrus Vinaigrette (page 171)
¾ cup pomegranate seeds
¼ cup honey goat cheese
¼ cup Garlic Confit (page 179)
1 cup chevdo (see Note)

I squeeze in clean meals as much as I can, and this satisfying salad packs in mega nutrients and flavor. Chaat is a type of street-style snack food that originated in India and normally has a crispy element paired with sweet and tangy flavors. This dish is so easy to prepare: use up whatever you have on hand in the fridge.

Bring a medium-sized pot of salted water to a gentle boil over medium-high heat. Meanwhile, fill a bowl with ice water. Add broccolini to the pot and cook for 1 minute. Using a slotted spoon, transfer to the bowl of ice water and gently stir. After 1 minute, remove to a baking sheet lined with a dish towel to drain.

Preheat a grill pan or BBQ to high heat. Remove dish towel from the baking sheet and drizzle broccolini with oil, then add salt and pepper. Toss to combine.

Grill broccolini for 3–4 minutes, turning as necessary to produce char marks. Transfer to the baking sheet and toss with citrus vinaigrette.

Transfer the broccolini to a serving plate, add pomegranate seeds, crumbled honey goat cheese and pieces of garlic confit, and sprinkle with chevdo.

NOTE: Chevdo is an Indian snack mix made up of dried ingredients and spices. It can be found at South Asian markets.

THE DO-GOOD-TASTE-GOOD SALAD

WITH CREAMY CUMIN-YOGURT DRESSING

SERVES 4–6

PICKLED BROCCOLI STALKS AND CELERY LEAVES

1 clove garlic, crushed

1 cup apple cider vinegar

1 Tbsp honey

1 tsp salt

¾ tsp black peppercorns

½ tsp black mustard seeds

½ cup broccoli stalks, cut into thin strips

1 cup celery leaves

CUMIN-YOGURT DRESSING

1 cup plain yogurt

2 Tbsp finely chopped cilantro

1 Tbsp finely chopped mint

1 tsp lemon zest

1 tsp cumin seeds, toasted and ground

1 tsp chaat masala

¾ tsp salt

1 Tbsp fresh lemon juice

2 tsp extra-virgin olive oil

½ tsp honey

SALAD

3 heads romaine lettuce, roughly chopped

1 unpeeled mango, cut into chunks (we eat the peel in this salad!)

1 red bell pepper, seeded, deveined and cut into thin strips

1 cup shredded red cabbage

½ cup roughly chopped herb stems

2 scallions, thinly sliced, plus extra for garnish

I am always seeking new and inventive ways to stretch out food supplies and utilize entire vegetables and proteins to ensure nothing is ever wasted. This recipe reveals how easy it can be to reduce food waste at home.

PICKLED BROCCOLI STALKS AND CELERY LEAVES In a small saucepan, combine garlic, vinegar, honey, salt, peppercorns and mustard seeds. Pour in 1 cup water, stir and bring to a simmer over medium heat. Remove from heat, then set aside to cool slightly. Add broccoli stalks and celery leaves and pickle for 1 hour. Drain, reserving pickling liquid for future pickling.

CUMIN-YOGURT DRESSING Combine all ingredients in a bowl and mix well.

SALAD In a large bowl, combine all ingredients. Stir in pickled broccoli stalks and celery leaves. Add 2 Tbsp cumin-yogurt dressing and toss. Transfer salad to a serving platter and top with additional dressing and scallions.

PINEAPPLE CHOW

SERVES 2–4

3 cloves garlic

2–3 Wiri Wiri chili peppers, to taste (see Note)

2 Tbsp roughly chopped culantro

2 Tbsp fresh lime juice

Salt and black pepper, to taste

1 pineapple, peeled, cored and cut into half moons

This Trinidadian spiced fruit dish is an absolute flavor bomb—and it couldn't be any simpler to make.

It combines unripe, semi-ripe and ripe fruit, which is then seasoned with fresh chili peppers, culantro (also known as sawtooth coriander, or chadon beni in Trinidad) and citrus juices. It's commonly prepared with mango, but I use pineapple as a tribute to the best pineapple I have ever eaten, which is found in Guyana. It's sweet, juicy and delectable. Go on then, it's time to chow down!

In a food processor, combine all ingredients, except pineapple, and blend well. Transfer the mixture to a bowl, add pineapple slices and refrigerate until needed.

> NOTE: Wiri Wiri chili peppers can be substituted with half the amount of Scotch bonnet or habanero chili peppers.

MASALA OATS

SERVES 2

¾ tsp ghee

½ tsp cumin seeds

¼ cup finely chopped red onion

½ tsp salt

1 Thai green chili pepper, thinly sliced

½ tomato, chopped

1 tsp Ginger-Garlic Paste (page 167)

½ tsp ground turmeric

½ tsp garam masala

⅔ cup quick oats

¼ cup finely chopped carrots

¼ cup thinly sliced sugar snap peas

2 Tbsp crispy fried onions, for garnish

Rise and shine, folks! Oats are a healthy way to kickstart the day, but this savory porridge takes a cue from India where such dishes are infused with warm spices and aromatics.

Heat ghee in a saucepan over medium-low heat. Add cumin seeds and fry for 15–20 seconds, until fragrant. Add red onion and salt and cook for 3–4 minutes, until onion is translucent.

Add chili pepper, tomato, ginger-garlic paste, turmeric and garam masala. Sauté for 1 minute. Increase heat to medium, then add oats and 1⅓ cups water. Bring to a gentle boil.

Stir in carrots and sugar snap peas and cook for 4–5 minutes, until the oatmeal is cooked through. Remove from the heat.

Transfer to bowls, top with crispy fried onions and serve warm.

GRILLED FRUIT SALAD
WITH FETA AND CHAAT MASALA VINAIGRETTE

SERVES 4

CHAAT MASALA VINAIGRETTE
1 small clove garlic, finely chopped

¼ cup grapeseed oil

3 Tbsp fresh lemon juice

1 Tbsp apple cider vinegar

1 Tbsp honey

1½ tsp Dijon mustard

1 Tbsp chaat masala

Salt and black pepper, to taste

GRILLED FRUIT SALAD
1 mango, cut into ¾-inch-thick slices

1 peach, cut into ¾-inch-thick slices

½ pineapple, cut into ¾-inch-thick slices

Grapeseed oil, for greasing and brushing

Salt and black pepper, to taste

4 cups assorted lettuce

1 cup strawberries, quartered

½ cup red seedless grapes, quartered vertically

½ cup blackberries, halved

1 cup crumbled feta

½ cup toasted pistachios

3 sprigs mint, leaves only, for garnish

CHAAT MASALA VINAIGRETTE Combine all ingredients in a squeeze bottle (or jar) and shake vigorously.

GRILLED FRUIT SALAD Preheat the BBQ to high heat.

Line a baking sheet with a dish towel or paper towels. Lay mango, peach and pineapple slices on the prepared baking sheet. Place another dish towel or paper towel on top, pressing down gently to remove excess moisture. This will help create grill marks.

Oil the grill. Brush oil on both sides of the fruit slices, then sprinkle with salt and pepper. Quickly add fruit to the BBQ and grill for 1 minute on each side, until grill marks are visible. Transfer to a large serving dish.

Add lettuce to the serving dish and drizzle with vinaigrette, then add strawberries, grapes, blackberries, feta and pistachios. Drizzle with more vinaigrette and garnish with mint.

SUPERFOOD PORRIDGE

SERVES 2–3

1 cup quinoa, soaked at least 2 hours or preferably overnight

2 green cardamom pods

1 cinnamon stick

¾ tsp finely chopped ginger

¼ tsp ground turmeric

¼ tsp black pepper

3½ cups 2% milk

2 Tbsp pumpkin seeds

2 Tbsp sunflower seeds

¾ cup quick oats

⅓ cup currants

1–2 Tbsp maple syrup

½ cup blueberries (divided)

1 Tbsp chia seeds

1 Tbsp hemp hearts

Sliced dates, for garnish (optional)

Breakfast is an essential for me because slow energy-releasing foods keep me sharp and alert for the day's activities, whether I'm presenting on a morning show, shooting for my socials or catering for hundreds. This superfood porridge is super easy to prepare and loaded with goodness.

Drain quinoa, then set aside.

In a medium saucepan, combine cardamom, cinnamon, ginger, turmeric and pepper. Pour in milk and bring to a simmer over medium heat.

Meanwhile, in a large frying pan, toast pumpkin and sunflower seeds over medium heat, until golden brown.

Add quinoa to the simmering milk and cook for 5 minutes. Stir in oats and currants and simmer for 2–3 minutes, until thickened. Remove from heat, fold in maple syrup and set aside to cool for 3 minutes.

Stir in most of the blueberries, reserving a few for garnish. Spoon porridge into bowls, then top with the reserved blueberries, toasted seeds, chia seeds, hemp hearts, and dates (if using). Serve immediately.

CURRIED SHAKSHUKA

SERVES 6

CURRIED SHAKSHUKA

2 Tbsp olive oil

1 tsp cumin seeds

1 onion, chopped

1 tsp salt

½ tsp black pepper

3 cloves garlic, finely chopped

2 Thai green or red chili peppers, thinly sliced

1 red bell pepper, seeded, deveined and chopped

1 Tbsp curry powder

1 tsp ground coriander

1½ tsp smoked paprika

3 cups tomato sauce

1 tsp sugar

1 cup roughly chopped spinach

2 tsp lemon juice

6 eggs

CILANTRO PESTO

1 cup chopped packed cilantro

¾ cup basil leaves

2 cloves garlic, finely chopped

2 Tbsp pine nuts

⅓ cup grated Parmigiano-Reggiano

⅓ cup olive oil

2 Tbsp fresh lemon juice

¾ tsp salt

ASSEMBLY

Crumbled feta, for garnish

Fresh herbs, for garnish

This family-style dish is the ultimate symbol of togetherness. Something so simple as sharing a meal with loved ones—and eating from the same dish—can be a powerful form of connection.

When I helped open a restaurant in Lahore, Pakistan, in 2023, the team prepared the staff meals together—we'd take quick stock of leftover ingredients and churn out a few delicious platters of food to serve the brigade. It was a frenzied and chaotic affair, but I would jump at the opportunity to relive it again. It was fun and spirited and notably elevated by the knowingness that we lived, worked and cooked in solidarity.

CURRIED SHAKSHUKA Heat oil in a large heavy-bottomed pan over medium heat. Add cumin seeds and fry for 1 minute, until fragrant. Add onion, salt and pepper and sauté for 3–4 minutes, until onion is lightly brown. Reduce heat to medium-low, then add garlic, chili peppers, bell pepper, curry powder, coriander and smoked paprika. Mix well.

Add the tomato sauce, sugar and ¾ cup water. Gently simmer for 10–15 minutes, until sauce has reduced and thickened.

Fold in spinach and lemon juice. Using the back of a spoon, create 6 divots in the sauce.

Crack eggs into each space, cover and steam for 5–8 minutes, depending on your desired doneness.

CILANTRO PESTO Combine all ingredients in a food processor and blend to desired consistency.

ASSEMBLY Remove shakshuka from the heat. Garnish with cilantro pesto, feta and fresh herbs. Serve.

MAYONNAISE

MAKES 1 CUP

1 large egg

2 tsp fresh lemon juice

1 tsp white wine vinegar

1 tsp Dijon mustard

¼ tsp salt

¾ cup grapeseed oil or Garlic Confit oil (page 179)

I can still remember the first time I learned how to make mayonnaise—I just found the emulsification of it so fascinating that I wanted to do it repeatedly. I then quickly realized how silky-smooth mayo could turn into a foundation for even more exciting condiments. Flavored mayos can be used in virtually any recipe that calls for mayonnaise—I love adding it to burgers and potato salads or using it as a dip for fries.

I tend to prepare mayonnaise by hand but, for the sake of ease, I have adapted the recipe so that it can be made with a hand blender or food processor. Mayo can be stored in an airtight container in the fridge for up to a week.

Combine all ingredients in a measuring jug.

Using an immersion blender, blend for 10–15 seconds at the base of the vessel, then gently move up and down until mixture is completely emulsified. Store in an airtight container in the fridge for up to a week.

Gochujang Mayo

Wasabi Mayo

Wiri Wiri
Mayo

Chipotle-Lime
Mayo

Curry Mayo

MAYO REMIX

HERB-LEMON MAYO

MAKES 1¼ CUPS

This vibrant mayo pairs beautifully with roasted chicken.

1 clove garlic, finely chopped
1 cup Mayonnaise (page 50)
2 tsp lemon zest
1 Tbsp finely chopped chives
1 Tbsp finely chopped dill
1 Tbsp finely chopped parsley
1 Tbsp finely chopped cilantro
2 tsp fresh lemon juice
½ tsp onion powder
½ tsp garlic powder
½ tsp salt
½ tsp black pepper

> NOTE: Wiri Wiri chili peppers can be substituted with half the amount of Scotch bonnet or habanero chili peppers.

WIRI WIRI MAYO

MAKES 1 CUP

Wiri Wiri chili peppers are an essential ingredient in Guyanese cooking and I can't praise them highly enough! The tangy little peppers have a distinct flavor and pack some intense heat. I like to serve this mayo with my Pepperpot Tacos (page 37) and my Salmon, Tuna and Plantain Poke Bowl (page 93).

1 cup Mayonnaise (page 50)
2–3 Wiri Wiri chili peppers, thinly sliced (see Note)
1 scallion, green part only, thinly sliced
½ tsp garlic powder
½ tsp onion powder
1 tsp fresh lemon juice
1 tsp lemon zest
Salt, to taste

CURRY MAYO

MAKES 1¼ CUPS

Curry mayo is especially delicious on burgers, fries, and potato salads and is excellent as a dip.

1 cup Mayonnaise (page 50)
2 tsp curry powder
½ tsp onion powder
½ tsp garlic powder
½ tsp honey
2 tsp fresh lemon juice

WASABI MAYO

MAKES ½ CUP

A zesty twist that is especially delicious with roasted vegetables.

½ cup Mayonnaise (page 50)
2 Tbsp wasabi paste
½ tsp ground ginger
¼ tsp salt

CHIPOTLE-LIME MAYO

MAKES 1¼ CUPS

Awaken your taste buds with this tasty condiment. Serve it on burgers or as a dip for veggies or dipping sauce for fries.

1 cup Mayonnaise (page 50)
¼ cup chipotle paste
1 Tbsp fresh lime juice
1 tsp lime zest
¼ tsp salt

GOCHUJANG MAYO

MAKES 1¼ CUPS

Gochujang is a fermented hot pepper paste that originates in Korea. It is sweet, salty, spicy, savory… and beyond words. I'm a fan of spicy foods, so it is a staple ingredient in my pantry. I like to slather this mayo on sandwiches, especially grilled cheeses. That's how you do it!

1 cup Mayonnaise (page 50)
¼ cup gochujang (Korean chili paste)

ALL RISE

Add   Mix   Cover

HOW TO

Flour   Cut   Fold

Heat   Ghee   Cook

Roll

Ghee

Spread

Tuck

Flatten

Roll

MAKE ROTI

Flip

Clap

Serve

SUGAR ROTI

MAKES 6

1½ cups flour, plus extra for dusting

½ tsp baking powder

¼ tsp salt

¼ cup (½ stick) butter, melted, plus extra for greasing and brushing

½ cup brown sugar

½ tsp ground cinnamon

½ tsp ground nutmeg

¼ tsp ground cardamom

My mom's sugar roti is a throwback to simpler times. The sweet scent of caramelized sugar and warm spices permeated the air; my brother Jai and I would bolt down the stairs and into the kitchen for first dibs. The deliciousness of sugar roti always tested the threshold of our patience: I'd take that impatient first bite before it was properly cooled down and burn my tongue on the hot filling. My mom would shake her head disapprovingly, as if to say, When will this child ever learn?

In a large bowl, combine flour, baking powder, salt and butter. Pour in ½ cup room temperature water and use your hand to mix and form a dough ball. Cover with a dish towel or wet paper towel and set aside for 20 minutes.

In a small bowl, combine brown sugar, cinnamon, nutmeg and cardamom.

Grease your hands with a little melted butter. Divide dough into 6 equal pieces and roll into balls. Dust with flour, then use your hands to form disks, each about 4 inches in diameter.

Brush each disk with a little butter, then top with sugar filling, dividing it between the 6 disks. Close a dough disk around the filling to make a ball. Roll the ball into a flat roti, about ⅛ inch thick, being careful to not burst the dough with the filling. Repeat with the remaining dough disks.

Heat a frying pan or tawa over medium heat. Add a roti and cook for 1 minute, flip and brush toasted side with butter. Cook for 1 minute, then turn over and brush second side with butter. Flip and cook for another minute, until beautifully browned on both sides. Transfer to a paper towel–lined plate. Set aside to cool for 5–10 minutes (trust me on this one), then enjoy.

OAT ROTI
WITH CUMIN AND FENUGREEK

MAKES 4–6

½ cup oats

2 Tbsp chickpea flour

1 tsp toasted cumin seeds

1 tsp dried fenugreek leaves
(*kasoori methi*)

½ tsp salt

Grapeseed oil, for greasing
and brushing

Gone are the days of bland gluten-free breads. Thanks to agricultural innovations and some creative ingenuity, delicious gluten-free breads of all shapes, sizes and flavors are made available at artisanal bakeries and finer supermarkets. And this tasty oat roti, punctuated with earthy, pungent cumin seeds and fenugreek leaves, is a worthy option.

Place oats in a blender and blend to a fine powder. Sift the oats through a fine-mesh sieve and discard any large pieces. Reserve ¼ cup for dusting.

In a large bowl, combine oat and chickpea flours, cumin seeds, fenugreek leaves and salt. Mix well. Gradually pour in ¾ cup hot water, stirring with a wooden spoon or spatula, until combined. Cover, then set aside to rest for 30 minutes.

Oil hands, then knead dough until it forms a ball. Lightly dust a clean work surface with oat flour. Divide dough into 4–6 portions, then flatten them into disks.

Heat a nonstick frying pan or tawa over medium-high heat. Using a rolling pin, roll out a roti, about ⅛ inch thick. Add roti to the pan and cook for 10–15 seconds. Flip, then brush roti with oil. Cook for 1–2 minutes, until lightly golden. Flip over again and brush with more oil. Fry for another 1–2 minutes, until lightly golden. Transfer to a plate, then cover with a dish towel to keep warm. Repeat with the remaining roti.

Serve warm.

GUYANESE PLAIT BREAD

MAKES 1 LOAF

¼ cup sugar

1 Tbsp active dry yeast

3½ cups flour, plus extra for dusting

1½ tsp salt

6 Tbsp melted butter (divided),
plus extra for greasing

Few aromas bring me as much joy as the smell of fresh plait bread—it's the scent of Christmas. It's traditionally served with Guyana's national dish, Pepperpot (page 127), but it's perfect for mopping up all kinds of stews, curries and soups.

In a bowl, combine sugar, yeast and 1½ cups warm water. Gently mix with a spoon. Cover with a dish towel and set aside for 10 minutes, until foamy.

In a stand mixer fitted with a hook attachment, combine flour, salt and 5 Tbsp melted butter. (You can also use your hands to mix everything in a bowl.) Pour in the yeast mixture. Mix on low speed for 5–6 minutes, until dough comes together. Remove dough from the mixer and shape into a ball with your hands. Transfer the dough ball to a greased bowl. Cover with a dish towel and set aside to rise for an hour, until doubled in size.

Grease a large baking sheet.

Transfer dough to a lightly floured work surface. Set aside ¼ cup of dough. (This will be used to make a decorative mini braid.) Divide the remaining dough into 3 equal parts. Roll each piece into an 18-inch length.

Secure the ends of the three pieces together. Braid the bread, then press the ends into themselves. Divide the reserved dough into three. Roll each piece to the length of the loaf, then braid the three strands together. Lay the thin braided cord down the middle of the loaf.

Transfer the loaf to the prepared baking sheet and set aside to proof for 45 minutes in a warm place. When it is almost ready to bake, preheat the oven to 375°F. Bake for 20–25 minutes, until golden brown.

Brush the top with the remaining 1 Tbsp of butter, then slice and serve.

KEEMA PARATHAS

SERVES 4

PARATHAS

1 cup flour

1 cup whole wheat flour, plus extra
for dusting

½ tsp baking powder

Pinch of salt

¼ cup ghee

KEEMA (see Note)

1 Tbsp grapeseed oil

1 onion, finely chopped

1 tsp salt

2 Tbsp Ginger-Garlic Paste (page 167)

1 lb ground beef, chicken or mutton

1 Tbsp Kashmiri chili powder

2 tsp ground coriander

¾ tsp ground turmeric

¾ tsp ground cumin

1 tsp garam masala

1 Tbsp fresh lemon juice

¼ cup finely chopped cilantro

ASSEMBLY

Grapeseed oil, for frying

Ghee, for brushing

Smoked Raita (page 177) or Green
Chutney (page 176), to serve (optional)

NOTE: Take care not to overstuff the
parathas with filling; otherwise, it'll
spill out everywhere.

Consider making a big batch of
keema—the recipe can be easily
doubled or tripled up, stored in
freezer bags and defrosted for quick
and easy meals.

I consumed my fair share of stuffed parathas during my travels across India and Pakistan. What's not to love about the combination of flatbreads and ground meat? Equally delicious are parathas stuffed with paneer or vegetables. The layered dough here is based on my mom's Roti (page 56), with perfectly soft and fluffy results.

PARATHAS Combine all ingredients, except ghee, in a bowl.

Form a well in the center, then slowly add ¾ cup water and mix with your fingers to form a dough. Cover with a damp paper towel and set aside to rest for 10 minutes. Divide dough into 6 equal pieces and roll into balls.

Dust a dough ball with whole wheat flour. Using a rolling pin, roll the ball into an 8-inch disk. Brush a thin layer of ghee over the disk and sprinkle with flour. Using a knife, make a straight cut from the center of the disk to the outside edge. Take one cut edge and fold it back over the dough. Fold over again and again, around the disk, until you create a cone shape. Tuck the tip into the center of the cone and wrap into a ball. (This will help ensure the layers don't separate when the dough is rolled out again.) Slightly flatten into a small disk and cover with a damp paper towel. Repeat with the remaining balls of dough. Set aside for 10–15 minutes. (For visual guidance, see the Roti recipe on page 58.)

KEEMA Meanwhile, heat oil in a large frying pan over medium-high heat. Add onion and salt and sauté for 5–7 minutes, until golden brown. Add ginger-garlic paste and sauté for 1–2 minutes, until aromatic.

Add ground meat and sauté for 3 minutes. Mix in spices, then pour in 1 cup water. Bring to a boil, then cover and reduce to medium-low heat. Simmer for 30 minutes, stirring occasionally, until water has reduced entirely.

Stir in lemon juice and cilantro. Season to taste. Set aside to cool.

ASSEMBLY On a work surface lightly dusted with whole wheat flour, roll out a piece of dough into a 4-inch disk. Dust with flour, then add ½ cup cooled filling to the center (see Note). Bring the edges together over the filling and pinch to seal. Lightly dust the paratha and work surface with more flour, set the paratha seam side down, then gently press dough to flatten it out. Carefully roll out to 5–6 inches in diameter. Place on a baking sheet lined with parchment paper. Repeat with the remaining dough and filling.

Heat a little oil in a griddle pan or tawa over medium-low heat. Add a paratha and fry for 1–2 minutes, until golden. Flip and brush with ghee. Fry for 1 minute and flip again, then brush with ghee. Repeat with the remaining parathas.

Serve hot straight from the pan, with raita or chutney if you wish.

GARLIC AND CILANTRO NAAN

MAKES 10–12

4 cups flour, plus extra for dusting

2 tsp active dried yeast

2 tsp sugar

1 tsp baking powder

1 tsp salt

1 cup whole milk, warm

¼ cup plain yogurt, room temperature

2 Tbsp grapeseed oil, plus extra
for brushing

1 egg, beaten

3 Tbsp butter, room temperature

2 cloves garlic, finely chopped

2 tsp chopped cilantro

I'm fascinated by the power of food and the way it can make us feel—the best dishes for me will satiate, evoke memory and impact my mood (for the better).

This soft and fluffy naan (or flatbread) does all that and more. It is peppered with fragrant garlic and cilantro, which can be enhanced with a distinctive charred flavor, courtesy of a tandoori oven. For the sake of ease, however, I've provided stovetop instructions. The naan makes a perfect vehicle for mopping up my hearty Butter Chicken (page 110). Trust me, you'll be generously rewarded for your efforts.

Put flour in a large bowl and create a well in the center. Add yeast, sugar, baking powder, salt, milk, yogurt, oil and egg. Using a wooden spoon, slowly mix in the flour until a dough is formed.

Lightly dust a clean work surface with flour, then knead the dough for 5 minutes. Brush dough surface with oil, transfer to a bowl and cover with a dish towel. Set aside and let rise for 1–2 hours, until doubled in size.

In a small bowl, combine butter, garlic and cilantro and set aside.

Tip dough ball onto the work surface. Slice into 10–12 pieces. Using a rolling pin, roll out dough into rounds or ovals, about ⅓ inch thick. Add flour to the rolling pin or work surface, if necessary, to prevent dough from sticking.

Brush a large frying pan with oil and heat over medium heat. Add naan and fry for 2 minutes, until golden brown or lightly charred. Flip, then brush the garlic butter over the cooked side. Fry for 1 minute. Transfer naan to a plate and cover with aluminum foil to keep warm. Repeat with the remaining naan. Serve warm.

ROMAINE CALM

VEGETARIAN

LITTLE INDIA MASALA CORN

SERVES 4

SEASONING
¾ tsp salt
1 tsp red chili powder
¾ tsp garlic powder
¾ tsp paprika
½ tsp ground cumin
¾ tsp amchur powder
½ tsp ground coriander
¼ tsp black pepper

STREET CORN
2 tsp grapeseed oil
4 ears corn, shucked
1 Tbsp butter
1 lime, cut into wedges
Chipotle-Lime Mayo (page 53), to serve

As a child, our family made regular trips to Little India in downtown Toronto. There, we would sip on chai and shop for clothes, books, CDs and Bollywood DVDs. But the highlight would be the pit stops at the snack vendors, particularly those who sold masala corn. The alluring scent of charred BBQ enticed me every time—I once ate four, to my mother's dismay.

These days, I don't visit Little India as much as I'd like. But when I do, I am instantly transported to those bygone days.

Preheat the BBQ to high heat.

Combine the seasoning ingredients in a small bowl.

Brush oil over corn. Add to the BBQ and grill for 5–6 minutes, until slightly charred on all sides.

Transfer corn to a plate, then brush with butter. Press a lime wedge into the seasoning blend, then brush it over a cob of corn, and repeat with the rest. Serve immediately with chipotle-lime mayo.

DESI GRILLED CHEESE
WITH GREEN CHUTNEY

SERVES 2

2 tsp grapeseed oil

1 small red onion, thinly sliced

½ tsp salt

2 tsp ghee

1½ tsp Ginger-Garlic Paste (page 167)

¾ tsp dried fenugreek leaves (*kasoori methi*)

½ tsp red chili powder

¼ tsp ground coriander

¼ tsp ground cumin

¼ tsp ground turmeric

2 Tbsp butter, room temperature

4 slices sourdough bread

1 cup grated sharp cheddar

¾ cup grated Gouda with cumin (see Note)

¾ cup grated smoked mozzarella

½ cup grated Asiago cheese

Green Chutney (page 176), to serve

Spices have the power to elevate dishes to the next level, and this classic is no exception to the rule. Here, a good ol' grilled cheese gets a spicy makeover with four types of cheese and the addition of chili powder, coriander and turmeric. Double down on flavor by adding a Gouda with cumin and serve it up with a tart green chutney for a delectable affair. Mad love.

Heat oil in a medium frying pan over medium heat. Add onion and salt and sauté for 6–7 minutes, until golden. Reduce heat to medium-low.

Add ghee, ginger-garlic paste, fenugreek leaves, chili powder, coriander, cumin, and turmeric. Sauté for another 1–2 minutes, then set aside.

Heat a large frying pan over medium-low heat. Butter both sides of the 4 bread slices. Place 2 slices in the pan and toast until golden. Flip and toast the other sides, then set aside. Repeat with the other 2 slices.

Reserve 2 Tbsp of each cheese and set aside. (This will be used to crust the sandwich after.)

Place 2 slices of toast back in the pan, and divide the cheddar between them. Top each with onion, Gouda, smoked mozzarella and Asiago. Place the 2 remaining slices of toast on top. Flip and fry for 1 minute.

Flip again, then sprinkle remaining cheese over both bread slices. Because the bread is warm, the cheese will adhere to it when patted down. Fry for 1–2 minutes, then flip again. (The cheese side is now down.) Fry for 3 minutes, until cheese around the edges turns golden brown. Flip and fry until the cheese filling has melted.

Slice sandwiches in half and serve with green chutney.

NOTE: Gouda is a semi-soft Dutch cheese, eponymously named after the town where it originated. Traditionally, it's smooth and creamy in color and flavor. Cumin seeds throughout the cheese add a spiced warmth. Find it at your local artisanal cheese shop.

GUYANESE-STYLE COOK-UP RICE

SERVES 6

4 tsp grapeseed oil

1 onion, finely chopped

2 tsp salt

1 tsp black pepper

5 cloves garlic, finely chopped

1–2 Wiri Wiri chili peppers, to taste (see Note)

2 stalks celery, chopped

2 scallions, finely chopped

1 carrot, finely chopped

1 bay leaf

2 Tbsp Green Seasoning (page 167)

1 Tbsp thyme leaves

1 tsp finely chopped ginger

1 (12-oz) can coconut milk

2 cubes vegetable bouillon

1 Tbsp cassareep

2 cups long-grain white rice, rinsed and drained

1 (15-oz) can red kidney beans or beans of your choice, rinsed and drained

2 cups spinach

Store-bought or homemade Hot Sauce (page 140), to serve

Every country seems to have a defining rice dish: Italy has risotto, China has congee, Spain has paella. And Guyana? We have cook-up rice. And what's not to love? I really enjoy preparing this dish for a crowd because it's LOADED with Caribbean flavor, it's prepared in one pot and it's cheap as chips to make. There's enough to go around for a large family, but it works for a party of two as well (#cookonceeattwice).

Heat oil in a large saucepan over medium heat. Add onion, salt and black pepper and sauté for 5–7 minutes, until golden brown. Add garlic, Wiri Wiri chili pepper(s), celery, scallions, carrot, bay leaf, green seasoning, thyme and ginger. Cook for 5–6 minutes.

Pour in coconut milk and 2¾ cups water, then add bouillon cubes and cassareep. Stir in rice, then reduce heat to medium-low and cover. Simmer for 15 minutes, or until cooked through.

Remove from heat. Fold in beans and spinach, and let stand until warmed through and spinach leaves have wilted.

Serve warm with hot sauce.

NOTE: Wiri Wiri chili peppers can be substituted with half the amount of Scotch bonnet or habanero chili peppers.

PALAK PANEER SPANA-KOPITA

MAKES 26–30

SPINACH AND PANEER FILLING
1 Tbsp ghee (divided)
1 cup grated Paneer (page 179)
1 tsp cumin seeds
1 onion, finely chopped
2 Tbsp Ginger-Garlic Paste (page 167)
2 tsp dried fenugreek leaves
(*kasoori methi*)
1 tsp ground coriander
¾ tsp garam masala
2 tsp Kashmiri chili powder
1 tsp ground turmeric
2½ tsp salt, plus extra to taste
¾ tsp amchur powder
½ tomato, chopped
16 cups chopped packed spinach,
well rinsed
½ cup chopped cilantro
1 cup crumbled feta cheese
1 cup chopped dill

ASSEMBLY
1 lb phyllo sheets
Melted butter, for brushing
Roasted Red Pepper Chimichurri (p. 178),
to serve

I can't resist a good spanakopita: the combination of flaky, buttery phyllo, earthy spinach and tangy feta brings me immense joy. But the reimagination of it with palak paneer makes my knees buckle.

This recipe is an unexpected pairing of classic Greek and Indian flavors. While it sounds unusual, the marriage works beautifully.

SPINACH AND PANEER FILLING Heat 2 tsp ghee in a large nonstick saucepan over medium heat. Add paneer and sauté for 4–5 minutes, until golden brown. Transfer to a plate.

In the same pan, heat the remaining 1 tsp of ghee and the cumin seeds and cook for 1 minute, until they begin to sputter. Add onion and sauté for 5–7 minutes, until softened and translucent. Stir in ginger-garlic paste and sauté for 1 minute, until fragrant.

Add fenugreek leaves, coriander, garam masala, chili powder, turmeric, salt, amchur powder and tomato and sauté for 2–3 minutes, until fragrant. Stir in spinach and cilantro. Pour in ½ cup water and simmer for 20 minutes, until thickened. The goal here is to have the mixture more dry than not. Set aside to cool completely.

Once cooled, roughly chop the spinach mixture, then fold in feta, paneer and dill. Season to taste with salt.

ASSEMBLY Preheat oven to 400°F. Line a baking sheet with parchment paper.

Cut phyllo sheets into 3 long strips. Arrange 3 strips of phyllo, side by side, on a cutting board. Brush the top side with butter. Lay another strip of phyllo atop each, then brush with butter. Add 1–2 Tbsp of spinach filling along the bottom. Fold the bottom corner over the filling to create a triangle. Continue to fold, until you have a triangular parcel. Place on the prepared baking sheet. Repeat with the remaining phyllo and filling—you should end up with 26–30 pieces.

Brush the top of each triangle with butter. Bake for 20 minutes, or until golden brown. Set aside to cool for 3 minutes, then serve with chimichurri.

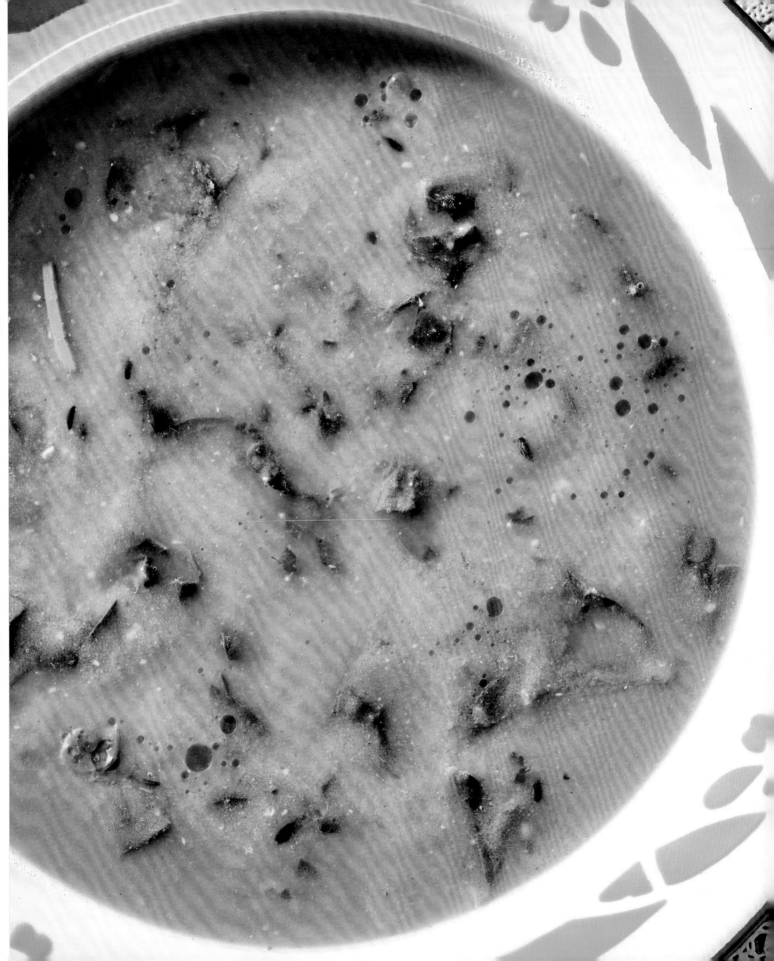

MOM'S DHAL

SERVES 4

DHAL
1 cup yellow split peas, rinsed

1 tsp salt

3 cloves garlic, finely chopped

1–2 Wiri Wiri chili peppers, to taste (see Note)

1 small white onion, finely chopped

1 scallion, chopped

1 tsp curry powder

½ tsp ground turmeric

½ tsp ground cumin, toasted

1 cup baby spinach leaves

CHUNKAY (see Note)
3 Tbsp grapeseed oil

1 tsp cumin seeds

1 clove garlic, thinly sliced

ASSEMBLY
Roti (page 56), to serve

When comfort calls, this humble dhal satisfies me like nothing else. As kids, my brother Jai and I would tear up fresh homemade Roti (page 56) and dip them into our dhal.

It's a simple dish with humble ingredients, often prepared whenever we needed a quick and hearty meal on the table. This heirloom recipe is a preservation of my cultural ancestry and, more importantly, an invaluable connection to my late grandmother. It's the perfect expression of my family.

DHAL Add 10 cups water to a large saucepan and bring to a gentle boil over medium heat. Stir in split peas and salt. Add garlic, Wiri Wiri chili pepper(s), onion, scallion, curry powder, turmeric and cumin. Mix well. Cover partially, then simmer for 35–40 minutes, until split peas are softened. Remove from heat.

Using an immersion blender, blend until smooth. Stir in spinach.

CHUNKAY Heat oil in a small skillet over medium-low heat. Add cumin seeds—they should sputter once they hit the oil. Cook for 30 seconds before adding garlic, then fry until golden brown.

ASSEMBLY Carefully pour the chunkay into the dhal. Cover with a lid and set aside for 2–3 minutes to trap the aromas. Stir, then serve with roti.

NOTES: Chunkay is a way of tempering aromatics before they're added to a dahl. East Indians have something similar called *tadka* or *parka*.

Wiri Wiri chili peppers can be substituted with half the amount of Scotch bonnet or habanero chili peppers.

GRILLED PANEER AND WATERMELON SANDWICH
WITH CILANTRO PESTO

SERVES 2

GRILLED PANEER AND WATERMELON
4 tsp grapeseed oil

8 oz Paneer (page 179), cut into
2 × 3-inch slices, ⅓ inch thick

4 slices watermelon, about ½ inch thick,
patted dry

1 tsp salt

1 tsp black pepper

CILANTRO PESTO
2 cloves garlic

1½ cups packed cilantro leaves

⅓ cup grated Parmigiano-Reggiano

2 Tbsp pine nuts

½ tsp salt

½ tsp black pepper

1 Tbsp fresh lemon juice

⅓ cup extra-virgin olive oil

ASSEMBLY
1 tsp butter

2 hamburger buns

Herb-Lemon Mayo (page 52)

1 cup arugula

¼ red onion, sliced

Aw, now this is sunshine on a plate—the flavor combo will blow your mind! Salty paneer, charred sweet watermelon and a vibrant pesto come together as an exciting filling in this refreshing summer sandwich you never knew you needed.

To get the best grill results, pat the watermelon dry before grilling.

GRILLED PANEER AND WATERMELON Preheat the BBQ to high heat.

Brush oil over paneer and watermelon. Season with salt and pepper. Add paneer and watermelon to the grill and sear for 2–3 minutes, until charred on both sides.

CILANTRO PESTO Combine all ingredients, except oil, in a food processor or blender. Pulse until incorporated and slightly chunky. Slowly drizzle in oil until emulsified. (Take care not to overblend it; otherwise, you'll heat the pesto.)

ASSEMBLY Lightly butter the cut sides of the hamburger buns. Place on the grill, buttered side down. Toast for 1–2 minutes, until golden brown.

Transfer buns to plates. Brush cut side of bottom buns with pesto and cut side of top buns with herb-lemon mayo. To each bottom bun, add a slice of watermelon, a slice of paneer, and another slice of watermelon, then top with arugula and red onion slices. Cover with top bun. Serve warm.

MOM'S OKRA

SERVES 2

4 cups okra

2 Tbsp grapeseed oil

1 red onion, finely chopped (1 cup)

6 cloves garlic, finely chopped

½ cup chopped tomato

1 Wiri Wiri chili pepper, finely chopped
(see Note)

1 Tbsp finely chopped ginger

½ tsp ground cumin

½ tsp amchur powder

½ tsp salt

Steamed rice or Roti (page 56), to serve

When we were young, I'd often find mom slicing okras and laying them out on a tray to dry out overnight. Why? I once asked. She explained that my grandmother taught her how to reduce okras' sliminess with this one simple technique.

Whenever she makes this signature dish of hers, she always dries out her okra. And I bet you can guess who followed suit.

Line a baking sheet with parchment paper. Wash okra, then pat dry well. Trim ends, then slice into ¾-inch rounds. Spread them out in a single layer on the prepared baking sheet and set aside overnight to dry out (and reduce the sliminess).

Heat oil in a large frying pan over medium-high heat. Add onion and sauté for 4–5 minutes until golden brown and crispy around some edges. Reduce heat to medium, then add garlic and tomato and sauté for 2–3 minutes.

Add okra, Wiri Wiri chili pepper, ginger, cumin, amchur powder and salt and cook for 15–20 minutes, until okra becomes slightly dry.

Transfer to a serving plate. Serve immediately with rice or roti.

NOTE: Wiri Wiri chili peppers can be substituted with half the amount of Scotch bonnet or habanero chili peppers.

METEMGEE WITH DUFF

SERVES 4

DUFF

1 Tbsp butter, room temperature, plus extra for greasing

1½ cups flour

2 Tbsp brown sugar

1 tsp baking powder

½ tsp salt

METEMGEE

2 Tbsp coconut oil

1 onion, finely chopped

2 tsp salt

1 tsp black pepper

2 Tbsp finely chopped garlic

2 Tbsp finely chopped ginger

2 Wiri Wiri chili peppers, chopped (see Note)

3 Tbsp Green Seasoning (page 167)

2 tsp thyme leaves, plus extra for garnish

4 cups coconut milk

1 lb cassava, peeled and cut into 2-inch chunks (see page 85)

1 lb sweet potato, peeled and cut into 2-inch chunks

1 lb yam, peeled and cut into 2-inch chunks

1 lb eddoe or taro, peeled and cut into 2-inch chunks (see Note)

2 yellow plantains, peeled and sliced

This popular Guyanese dish is enjoyed across the Caribbean, and the best versions are prepared with fresh coconut milk and root vegetables. It warms my heart, soothes my soul and satisfies my most-needed comfort food cravings.

The pillowy steamed dumplings known as duff help soak up the inviting broth and make for a happy belly—have no fear, they're super easy to make.

DUFF Grease a baking sheet.

Combine all ingredients in a bowl. Using your hands, rub butter into dough until it forms pea-sized crumbs. Create a well in the middle of the bowl, then add ½ cup warm water.

Knead for 1–2 minutes in the bowl until the dough is soft and pliable. If necessary, add more water, 1 tsp at a time. Cover with a damp dish towel and set aside for 30 minutes.

Divide dough into 8 pieces. On a lightly dusted work surface, roll a piece of dough into a 1 × 3-inch oval shape. (It doesn't need to be perfect—this is home cooking!) Place on the prepared baking sheet and cover with a damp dish towel. Repeat with the remaining pieces.

METEMGEE Heat oil in a large pot over medium heat. Add onion, salt and black pepper and sauté for 4–5 minutes, until lightly golden brown. Add garlic and ginger and sauté for another minute.

Stir in Wiri Wiri chili peppers, green seasoning and thyme. Pour in coconut milk and 5 cups water. Stir to combine, then bring to a gentle boil. Add cassava, sweet potato, yam and eddoe (or taro) and gently boil for 15 minutes, until tender.

Stir in plantains and cook for 5 minutes before carefully laying duff on top of the mixture in a single layer. Reduce heat to medium-low and cover. Steam for 8 minutes, without opening the lid—the duff will cook and puff up.

Garnish with thyme and serve warm.

NOTE: Eddoe is a tropical fruit with a thick stem, and is related to taro.

Wiri Wiri chili peppers can be substituted with half the amount of Scotch bonnet or habanero chili peppers.

HOW TO PREP CASSAVA

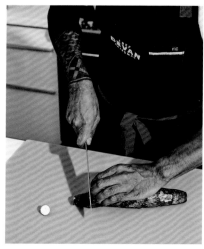

Trim ends of cassava, then slice into 2-3 inch pieces.

Using a paring knife, create a ⅛-inch slit in the skin.

Place knife carefully under the skin and peel it back.

Boil for 15-20 minutes, until fork tender.

Carefully remove the vein.

Duff

Metemgee
with Duff
(P. 84)

A SHORE THING

FISH & SEAFOOD

FISH CAKES
WITH MANGO SOUR

SERVES 6–8

FISH CAKES

1 lb saltfish (salted cod)

4 cloves garlic, finely chopped

2 Wiri Wiri chili peppers (see Note)

½ onion, finely chopped

2 scallions, sliced

1 egg

2 cups mashed potato or cassava
(see page 85)

½ tsp black pepper

2 tsp smoked paprika

½ tsp onion powder

½ tsp garlic powder

ASSEMBLY

1 cup vegetable oil

Mango Sour (page 175), to serve

Lime wedges, to serve

If you've ever had fish tacos with mango salsa, you'll know that fish and refreshing citrus flavors make a winning combination. This classic Guyanese dish is no different. The fish cakes are deep-fried to crisp perfection and served with a piquant mango sour. When purchased at roadside stalls in Guyana, they are often wrapped in a thin flatbread called puri. They make a popular afterschool snack for kiddos.

FISH CAKES Soak saltfish in a bowl of water for 1 hour. Drain, then add saltfish to a pot of gently boiling water and gently boil for 5 minutes. Drain, then set aside to cool. Using your hands, flake fish into small pieces.

In a large bowl, combine the saltfish and the remaining ingredients and mix well with your hands.

Shape fish mixture into 2½-inch pucks, about ½ inch thick. Makes 14 cakes.

ASSEMBLY Heat oil in a deep saucepan over medium heat. Working in batches to avoid overcrowding, carefully lower fish cakes into the pan and fry for 3–4 minutes on each side, until golden brown. Using a slotted spoon, transfer to a paper towel–lined plate. Repeat with the remaining fish cakes.

Serve immediately with mango sour and lime wedges.

NOTE: Wiri Wiri chili peppers can be substituted with half the amount of Scotch bonnet or habanero chili peppers.

SALMON, TUNA AND PLANTAIN POKE BOWL

WITH NORI AND WIRI WIRI MAYO

SERVES 4

2 cups black rice (forbidden rice)

1 cup cubed sushi-grade salmon

1 cup cubed sushi-grade tuna

1 mango, finely chopped

½ cucumber, chopped (1 cup)

1 cup cooked edamame

3 Tbsp Ginger-Soy Glaze (page 168) (divided)

Salt and black pepper, to taste

½ cup Wiri Wiri Mayo (page 52)

1 avocado, thinly sliced (optional)

1 cup Fried Plantains (page 20)

2 Tbsp wasabi peas

2 sheets nori, thinly sliced (julienned)

½ tsp shichimi togarashi

A good poke bowl will leave you feeling satiated but not incapacitated. You can also customize it by adding your favorite toppings: chopped cucumber, thinly sliced radishes, chopped nori, mango, sesame seeds. The best part? You really can't go wrong.

Add rice to a saucepan and fill halfway with water. Boil for 20 minutes, until cooked through. Drain, then set aside.

In a bowl, combine salmon, tuna, mango, cucumber, edamame and 1 Tbsp ginger-soy glaze and season with salt and pepper. Toss to combine.

To serve, scoop rice into bowls. Drizzle with the remaining 2 Tbsp ginger-soy glaze. Top with salmon mixture. Drizzle with Wiri Wiri mayo, then garnish with fanned avocado (if using), fried plantains, wasabi peas, nori and shichimi togarashi.

CARIBBEAN CEVICHE

SERVES 4

LECHE DE TIGRE

1 Tbsp aji amarillo paste or
¼ habanero chili pepper

2–3 cloves garlic

1 tsp chopped ginger

½ stalk celery

⅛ red onion

1 Tbsp Green Seasoning (page 167)

¾ cup fresh lime juice

¾ cup fresh lemon juice

2 Tbsp evaporated milk

4 tsp honey

1½ tsp salt, plus extra to taste

2 oz best-quality white fish

2 sprigs cilantro, chopped

CEVICHE

1 cup peeled and cubed sweet potato,
in ½-inch cubes

8 oz best-quality white fish, diced

4 oz best-quality bay scallops, chopped

4 oz best-quality raw small shrimp,
peeled, deveined and chopped

1½ tsp salt, plus extra to taste

½ tsp pepper

¼ large red onion, thinly sliced and
rinsed under cold water (to remove
pungency), for garnish

1 small avocado, peeled and diced,
for garnish

Cancha or choclo (see Note),
for garnish (optional)

In 2016, I spent a month in Peru and worked at a local cevicheria in Lima. There, I learned to make leche de tigre, the citrus-based marinade used to cure fish. This is also where I discovered that a ceviche is only as good as the quality of the fish. Use the best you can find—it'll be worth it.

Aji amarillo is a fruity yet fiery orange-yellow Peruvian chili pepper. If you cannot find it, use a quarter of a habanero. The green seasoning introduces a Caribbean twist to this classic.

LECHE DE TIGRE In a blender, combine all ingredients, except cilantro, and blend well. Add cilantro and pulse several times. Season to taste with salt.

CEVICHE Bring a small saucepan of water to a boil. Add sweet potato and boil for 10 minutes, until tender. Drain and set aside to cool.

In a large bowl, combine fish, scallops, shrimp, salt and pepper. Toss to mix. Pour in 1 cup leche de tigre and 2 ice cubes and mix well. Season to taste with salt and set aside for 5 minutes, until the exterior of the chopped fish is opaque.

To plate, spoon ceviche into a bowl. Garnish with sweet potato, red onion, avocado and cancha (or choclo), if using.

NOTE: Cancha are Peruvian corn nuts and choclo is Peruvian corn. Both can be found at Latin supermarkets.

BAKE AND SALTFISH

SERVES 4

SALTFISH
1 lb saltfish (salted cod)

2 tsp vegetable oil

2 onions, finely chopped (2 cups)

½ tsp salt

4 cloves garlic, finely chopped

1 small stalk celery, finely chopped
(½ cup)

1 Tbsp tomato paste

½ tsp black pepper

2 scallions, thinly sliced

1 Wiri Wiri chili pepper (see Note)

1 tsp thyme leaves

3–4 tomatoes, chopped (1½ cups)

BAKE
2 cups flour, plus extra for dusting

1 cup whole wheat flour

2 Tbsp sugar

1 Tbsp baking powder

1 tsp salt

¼ cup (½ stick) butter, room
temperature

1½ cups 2% milk

⅓ cup shredded carrots

Grapeseed oil, for frying

This is a classic Guyanese breakfast! As a kid I loved to sleep in, but if there was one thing that would get me up early, it was the aroma of fresh-made bake and saltfish. I'd tear the fresh fried dough pocket in half, and steam would come wafting out. The saltiness combined with beautiful aromatics was a perfect pairing. This is my mother's recipe with a few tweaks of my own.

SALTFISH Put saltfish into a saucepan and cover with water. Gently boil for 10 minutes, then discard water. Repeat, but gently boil for only 5 minutes. Drain, then transfer to a bowl. Using a fork, flake fish.

Heat oil in a large frying pan over medium heat. Add onion and salt and sauté for 7 minutes, until lightly golden. Add garlic, celery, tomato paste and black pepper and sauté for another 2 minutes, until fragrant.

Add saltfish, scallions, Wiri Wiri chili pepper and thyme and mix well. Stir in tomatoes, reduce heat to low and cook for 10 minutes, until flavors meld. Remove from heat and set aside.

BAKE In a bowl, combine flours, sugar, baking powder and salt and mix well. Using your hands, work in butter until there is a crumbly texture.

In a blender, combine milk and carrots and blend until smooth. Reserve ¼ cup, then add the rest to the flour mixture. Mix, then knead dough until it comes together. If necessary, add some of the reserved milk mixture to bind the dough.

Cover dough ball with a damp paper towel and set aside to rest for 30 minutes.

Heat oil in a large frying pan, no more than a third deep, over medium-low heat, until it reaches a temperature of 350°F.

Lightly dust a work surface with flour. Using a rolling pin, roll out dough, about ¼ inch thick. Cut into 4-inch triangles. Working in batches, add to pan and fry for 1–2 minutes on each side, until golden brown. Makes 15–20 pieces.

ASSEMBLY Serve this dish as you would a curry with roti. A couple bake with a spoon of saltfish on top will set the world on fire.

> NOTE: Wiri Wiri chili peppers can be substituted with half the amount of Scotch bonnet or habanero chili peppers.

CARIBBEAN RISOTTO
WITH CRISPY SALMON

SERVES 4

MARINATED SALMON
4 (3-oz) skin-on salmon fillets
1 Tbsp Ginger-Garlic Paste (page 167)

RISOTTO
3½ cups vegetable stock
1 Tbsp olive oil
½ onion, finely chopped
¾ tsp salt, plus extra to taste
2 cloves garlic, finely chopped
½ Scotch bonnet chili pepper, finely diced
¾ tsp thyme leaves
½ tsp ground allspice
1 cup arborio rice
1 cup dry white wine
1 cup coconut milk
¼ cup finely chopped mango
2 tsp finely chopped red bell pepper
¼ cup finely grated Parmigiano-Reggiano
1 tsp butter
Black pepper, to taste

HERB SALAD
½ cup cilantro leaves
½ cup sliced scallions, sliced on a bias
½ cup mint leaves, torn
½ cup finely chopped chives
2 tsp lemon juice
2 tsp olive oil

ASSEMBLY
2 tsp olive oil
Salt, to taste
1–2 tsp Parmigiano-Reggiano
Lemon wedges, to serve

MARINATED SALMON Place salmon fillets skin side down on a sheet of paper towel–this will ensure the skin stays completely dry. Evenly brush the ginger-garlic paste onto the salmon flesh. Set aside to marinate.

RISOTTO Bring stock to a simmer in a medium saucepan.

Heat oil in a nonstick frying pan over medium heat. Add onion and salt and sauté for 7 minutes, until onion is translucent. Add garlic, chili pepper, thyme and allspice and sauté for another minute, until fragrant.

Add rice and sauté for 1–2 minutes, until lightly toasted. Pour in wine and simmer for 7 minutes, or until most of the wine has been absorbed. Ladle in ½ cup stock and stir until nearly all the liquid has been absorbed. Repeat until all the stock is used. Add coconut milk and cook for another 2–3 minutes, or until the rice is al dente.

Stir in mango, bell pepper, Parmigiano-Reggiano and butter. Season to taste with salt and black pepper.

HERB SALAD Meanwhile, combine all ingredients and set aside.

ASSEMBLY Meanwhile, heat oil in a frying pan over medium heat. Add salmon, skin side down, and season to taste with salt. Gently press on the fillet with a spatula for 30 seconds so the skin maintains contact with the pan. Cook for 2–3 minutes, until skin is golden brown. Turn over and cook for 1 minute. Turn off heat and allow salmon to continue cooking in the residual heat for another 1–2 minutes. Set aside until risotto is ready.

Spoon risotto onto individual plates. Top with salmon, crispy skin side up, then sprinkle with Parmigiano-Reggiano. Add herb salad and serve immediately with lemon wedges.

GUYANESE-STYLE PEPPER SHRIMP

SERVES 2

Grapeseed oil, for deep-frying

1 lb medium (21/25) shrimp, peeled and deveined

3 Tbsp cornstarch

1¼ tsp salt (divided), plus extra to taste

2 tsp sesame oil

3 cloves garlic, finely chopped

2 scallions, roughly chopped (divided)

1 (1-inch) piece ginger, finely chopped

3 Wiri Wiri chili peppers, finely chopped (see Note)

¼ small red onion, finely chopped

¼ red bell pepper, seeded, deveined and finely chopped

Fried curry leaves (optional), for garnish

Lime wedges, to serve

Store-bought or homemade Hot Sauce (page 140), to serve

Line a baking sheet with paper towel.

Add enough grapeseed oil to fill up a third of a large saucepan. Heat oil over medium-high heat until it reaches a temperature of 375°F.

In a bowl, combine shrimp, cornstarch and ¾ tsp salt. Toss well. Carefully lower shrimp into the pan, taking care not to splash hot oil. Deep-fry for 1–2 minutes, until golden brown. Transfer to the prepared baking sheet to drain excess oil.

Heat sesame oil in a wok or large frying pan over medium-high heat. Add garlic, half the scallions, ginger, Wiri Wiri chili peppers, onion and bell pepper. Season with the remaining ½ tsp salt. Toss well to combine.

Add shrimp and mix well. Season to taste with salt.

Transfer to a serving platter and garnish with the remaining scallions and fried curry leaves (if using). Serve warm with lime wedges and hot sauce.

NOTE: Wiri Wiri chili peppers can be substituted with half the amount of Scotch bonnet or habanero chili peppers.

GUYANESE PUMPKIN AND SHRIMP

SERVES 4

2 Tbsp grapeseed oil (divided)

¼ lb baby shrimp, peeled and deveined (if needed)

1 tsp salt (divided)

½ tsp black pepper (divided)

1 onion, finely chopped (¾ cup)

2 Tbsp Green Seasoning (page 167)

3 cloves garlic, finely chopped

1–2 Wiri Wiri chili peppers, to taste, finely chopped (see Note)

2 tsp brown sugar (optional)

1 tsp thyme leaves

½ tsp ground cumin

3 cups diced sugar pumpkin

1 scallion, roughly chopped

This heartwarming and soul-nourishing dish is served at religious ceremonies and functions—and it is so delicious. In Guyana, it is prepared with white belly shrimp, but you can use any type of shrimp for a touch of island authenticity at home.

Heat 1 Tbsp oil in a large saucepan over high heat. Add shrimp, ½ tsp salt and ¼ tsp black pepper and sauté for 1–2 minutes, until shrimp is slightly opaque. Transfer to a plate and set aside.

Heat the remaining 1 Tbsp oil in the same pan over medium heat. Add onion, green seasoning and the remaining ½ tsp salt. Sauté for 6–7 minutes, until onion is golden brown.

Stir in garlic, Wiri Wiri chili pepper(s), brown sugar (if using), thyme, cumin and the remaining ¼ tsp black pepper. Sauté for 2–3 minutes. Add pumpkin and stir to combine. Partially cover and simmer for 20–25 minutes, stirring frequently to prevent burning, until pumpkin is softened and cooked down. Add shrimp for the last 5 minutes of cooking. Remove from heat and fold in scallion. Serve warm.

NOTE: Wiri Wiri chili peppers can be substituted with half the amount of Scotch bonnet or habanero chili peppers.

JERK SHRIMP LETTUCE WRAPS

WITH APPLE, PEACH AND MANGO SALSA

SERVES 4

JERK SHRIMP
1 lb medium (21/25) shrimp, peeled and deveined

¼ cup + 1 Tbsp Jerk Marinade (page 169)

2 tsp grapeseed oil

APPLE, PEACH AND MANGO SALSA
1 clove garlic, finely chopped

1 tsp finely chopped cilantro

1 tsp fresh lime juice

¾ tsp honey

½ tsp lime zest

1 tsp grapeseed oil

½ tsp salt

¼ tsp black pepper

1 mango, finely chopped

1 peach, stoned and finely chopped

1 apple, cored and finely chopped

ASSEMBLY
1–2 Tbsp grapeseed oil

8 large iceberg, romaine or butter lettuce leaves

Scotch bonnet chili peppers, thinly sliced, for garnish (optional)

1 Tbsp toasted sesame seeds, for garnish

Originating in Jamaica, jerk seasoning is a flavorful blend of herbs and spices, chili peppers, allspice, thyme, cinnamon and nutmeg. Its most recognizable usage is in the eponymous dish, jerk chicken. It's my favorite spice blend and encapsulates my cooking style: bold, spiced and super versatile.

Here, I use it to season shrimp to create tasty lettuce wraps with plenty of crunchy goodness. Pair them with this refreshing salsa for a delectable meal of the tropics.

JERK SHRIMP In a bowl, combine all ingredients and mix well.

APPLE, PEACH AND MANGO SALSA In a bowl, combine all ingredients and mix well.

ASSEMBLY Heat oil in a frying pan over medium heat. Add shrimp and sear for 2–3 minutes on each side, until golden brown.

Place lettuce leaves on plates. Add shrimp, then top with salsa and chili peppers (if using) and sprinkle with sesame seeds. Serve.

KERALAN FISH CURRY

SERVES 2

MARINATED WHITE FISH
2 Tbsp Ginger-Garlic Paste (page 167)
¾ tsp ground turmeric
1 tsp Kashmiri chili powder
1 tsp salt
½ lb white fish, cut into chunks

FISH CURRY
2 Tbsp coconut oil
½ tsp black mustard seeds
Handful of fresh curry leaves
2 Thai green chili peppers, finely chopped
1 large onion, chopped (1 cup)
½ tsp salt
¼ tsp black pepper
2 Tbsp finely chopped garlic
1 Tbsp finely chopped ginger
1 Tbsp dried fenugreek leaves (*kasoori methi*)
½ tsp Kashmiri chili powder
1 tsp ground coriander
½ tsp ground turmeric
2 tsp tamarind purée
1 cup coconut milk
½ tsp sugar
Steamed brown rice, to serve

Some of my fondest culinary memories were in Kerala, the southernmost state of India renowned for its shoreline, coffee and spice plantations, and wildlife. Coconut, mustard seeds and curry leaves are prevalent in the cuisine, and I sometimes find myself reminiscing about those glorious aromatic scents in the air. I hope to transport you there with this dish.

MARINATED WHITE FISH Combine marinade ingredients in a medium bowl. Add fish and gently massage marinade into the flesh. Cover and refrigerate for 30 minutes to 1 hour.

FISH CURRY Heat oil in a saucepan over medium heat. Add mustard seeds and curry leaves and cook until they begin to sizzle and gently sputter. Add chili peppers, onion, salt, black pepper, garlic and ginger and sauté for 7–8 minutes, until golden brown.

Add fenugreek leaves, Kashmiri chili powder, coriander and turmeric and cook for 1–2 minutes. Add tamarind purée, then pour in coconut milk and 1 cup water.

Simmer for 15–20 minutes. Add sugar.

Add marinated fish, cover and simmer for 8–10 minutes, until cooked through.

Serve with steamed brown rice.

CHOP, CHOP, CHOP!

HOW TO BUILD A BETTER SALAD

I've always been praised for unique and inventive salads, but I wish I could take all the credit—much of it has to do with the bounty of ingredients I have access to. And you do as well!

Here, I've provided my framework for salad development. What many people don't realize is that salads are one of the easiest things to pull off with a little practice. It's a balance of tastes (salty, sweet, spicy) and textures (crispy, soft, crunchy, creamy).

This is the perfect opportunity for home cooks to produce something creative, original and absolutely tasty. Use a combination of what I've listed below or take a leap of faith and create something entirely new. In all my years of cooking, I've come to realize that risk-taking is part of the process in making a new discovery. Trial-and-error is an inherent part of the process and will help you become a better, more efficient cook! The results may just surprise you.

And when you've made a crazy tasty plate of food, you've got to share it with me on my socials. One of my greatest joys is to see home cooks become more confident in the kitchen.

All About the Base

ARUGULA
BUTTER LETTUCE
ENDIVE
KALE
MIXED GREENS
RADICCHIO
ROMAINE
SPINACH
SPRING MIX
TREVISO

Crunch Time

APPLE
BROCCOLI
CABBAGE
CAULIFLOWER
CELERY
CUCUMBER
FENNEL
ONION
POMEGRANATE
RADISH
RED PEPPER

Grain Power

BULGHUR/FALAFEL
CHICKPEAS
COUSCOUS
FARRO
FREEKEH
LENTILS
QUINOA
RICE

Soft Rocks

AVOCADO
BERRIES
CAPERS
CORN
DRIED FRUIT
EDAMAME
GRAPEFRUIT
GRAPES
JALAPENO
MANGO
MELON
MUSHROOM
OLIVES
ORANGE
ROASTED SWEET POTATO
TOMATO

The Protein Shake-Up

BEANS
CHEESE
CHICKEN
EGGS
HAM
LEAN STEAK
SALMON
TEMPEH
TOFU
TUNA
TURKEY

And to Top It Off...

BACON
CROUTONS
HERBS
NUTS
PITA CHIPS
SEEDS (CHIA, HEMP, PUMPKIN)
SEV (CRUNCHY INDIAN NOODLES)
TORTILLA CHIPS

Crowning Glory

NORI
NUTRITIONAL YEAST
SHICHIMI TOGARASHI
SUMAC
TAJÍN SEASONING

Dress to Impress

CASSAREEP DRESSING
(PAGE 172)
CHAAT MASALA VINAIGRETTE
(PAGE 44)
CITRUS VINAIGRETTE
(PAGE 171)
CREAMY FETA DRESSING
(PAGE 173)
CUMIN-YOGURT DRESSING
(PAGE 42)
SPICY CAESAR DRESSING
(PAGE 171)

A CUT ABOVE

MEAT & POULTRY

BUTTER CHICKEN

SERVES 2–3

MARINATED CHICKEN
¼ cup plain yogurt

1½ Tbsp fresh lemon juice

1 Tbsp Ginger-Garlic Paste (page 167)

1 tsp red chili powder

1 tsp garam masala

2 lbs boneless chicken,
cut into bite-sized pieces

1 Tbsp grapeseed oil

SAUCE
1 Tbsp ghee

1 Tbsp butter

3 green cardamom pods

1 black cardamom pod

1 small cinnamon stick

1 small star anise

1 tsp cumin seeds

1 onion, chopped

½ cup whole cashews

1½ Tbsp Ginger-Garlic Paste (page 167)

1 Tbsp dried fenugreek leaves
(kasoori methi)

1 tsp red chili powder

1 tsp garam masala

1 tsp ground coriander

¾ tsp ground turmeric

2 cups tomato purée (passata)

2 tsp sugar

Salt, to taste

ASSEMBLY
Chopped cilantro, for garnish

Steamed rice or Garlic and Cilantro
Naan (page 66), to serve

Want to add excitement to everyday eating? Read on. This recipe on my **Chef Dev at Home** *Instagram series went viral at the beginning of the pandemic. The ingredient list may seem long, but this recipe is all about building layer upon layer of deep, balanced flavor. People often tell me that it's become a mainstay in their repertoire. That's the best compliment I could ever receive.*

MARINATED CHICKEN In a large bowl, combine all ingredients, except chicken and oil. Add chicken and mix until well coated. Allow to marinate in the fridge for at least 1 hour, but preferably overnight for best results.

Preheat a grill pan or BBQ to medium-high. Add oil and grill chicken, turning occasionally, until it reaches an internal temperature of 150°F. (It will finish cooking in the sauce.) Set aside.

SAUCE Melt ghee and butter in a large saucepan over medium-low heat. Add cardamom pods, cinnamon, star anise and cumin seeds. Toast for 1–2 minutes, until fragrant.

Add onion, cashews, ginger-garlic paste and spices. Sauté for 3–4 minutes.

Add tomato purée, sugar and ½ cup water. Cook for 10 minutes. Transfer mixture to a blender and blend until smooth. Return the sauce back to the pan.

Fold grilled chicken into the sauce. Simmer for 10–15 minutes to meld the flavors. Season to taste with salt.

ASSEMBLY Garnish with cilantro. Serve over steamed rice or with naan bread.

HAKKA-STYLE CHILI CHICKEN

SERVES 2–4

CHICKEN

1 lb boneless, skinless chicken thighs, cut into bite-sized pieces

2 tsp finely chopped garlic

¾ cup potato or rice starch

2 tsp soy sauce

1 egg, beaten

Salt and black pepper, to taste

2 cups vegetable oil, for frying

CHILI SAUCE

1 Tbsp sesame oil

1 small onion, finely chopped

½ tsp salt, plus extra to taste

5–6 Thai green chili peppers, finely chopped

2 tsp finely chopped garlic

1 (1-inch) piece ginger, peeled and grated

1 small carrot, thinly sliced into rounds

1 stalk celery, thinly sliced

½ red bell pepper, seeded, deveined and chopped

1 Tbsp Chinese rice wine vinegar

1 Tbsp soy sauce

2 tsp honey

1 Tbsp cornstarch

2 Tbsp finely chopped scallions, for garnish

Steamed rice, to serve

Hakka cuisine is an amalgamation of Chinese and East Indian cuisines. It's characterized as quick to prepare and loaded with texture and flavor.

My brother first introduced me to Hakka cuisine. He was always on the search for the most authentic food—and the best places always seemed to be off the beaten track or complete holes-in-the-wall.

CHICKEN In a large bowl, combine all ingredients except oil. Allow to marinate in the fridge for at least 1 hour, but preferably overnight.

Heat oil in a deep fryer or large saucepan over medium-high heat until it reaches 350°F. Carefully lower chicken into the pan, taking care not to splash hot oil. Deep-fry for 4–5 minutes, until golden brown. Work in batches, if necessary, to avoid overcrowding. Transfer chicken to a paper towel–lined plate to drain excess oil. Set aside.

CHILI SAUCE Heat oil in a wok or large frying pan over medium-high heat. Add onion and salt and sauté for 2–3 minutes, until lightly golden brown. Add chili peppers, garlic and ginger and sauté for 1 minute. Add carrot, celery and bell pepper and sauté for another minute. Transfer to a plate.

In the same pan, combine vinegar, soy sauce, honey and 1 cup water.

In a small bowl, combine cornstarch and 4 tsp cold water and mix. (This is called a slurry.) Add slurry to the pan and simmer until thickened. Season to taste with salt.

Add chicken and the sautéed vegetables and toss well.

Transfer to a serving plate. Garnish with scallions and serve warm with rice.

PEPPERPOT WINGS

SERVES 4

¼ cup cassareep

1 tsp onion powder

1 tsp garlic powder

1 tsp ground ginger

1 tsp ground allspice

¾ tsp ground cloves

½ tsp ground cinnamon

2 Tbsp brown sugar

4–5 sprigs thyme, leaves only,
plus extra for garnish

2 Wiri Wiri chili peppers (see Note)

2 lbs chicken wings

Zest of 1 orange, plus extra for garnish

Grapeseed oil, for greasing

I am always looking for new ways to rework my favorite childhood recipes. This modernization of a historic Guyanese dish (page 127) brings the wonderful flavors of my homeland to any party—and I love it especially during Super Bowl celebrations.

In a bowl, combine cassareep, onion and ginger powders, and spices. Mix well, then add brown sugar, thyme and Wiri Wiri chili peppers. Using an immersion blender, blend until smooth. (Alternatively, use a food processor or blender.)

Transfer the mixture to a bowl, then add wings and orange zest and mix well to evenly coat. Set aside to marinate for at least 1 hour, or preferably overnight in the fridge.

Preheat a grill pan or BBQ to medium heat and grease with oil. Grill wings for 20–25 minutes, basting with the leftover marinade for the first 15 minutes of cooking time. Cook wings until the internal temperature reaches 160–165°F.

Pile up wings on a serving plate and garnish with thyme leaves and orange zest. Serve immediately.

NOTE: Wiri Wiri chili peppers can be substituted with half the amount of Scotch bonnet or habanero chili peppers.

MOM'S CHICKEN STEW

SERVES 4

2 Tbsp grapeseed oil

6 cloves garlic, finely chopped

2 tomatoes, chopped

1 onion, chopped (1 cup)

1 small stalk celery, chopped (½ cup)

1 Wiri Wiri chili pepper, finely chopped
(see Note), plus extra whole chili peppers
(optional) for garnish

2 lbs bone-in chicken thighs, cut into
2-inch pieces

2½ tsp salt

5 basil leaves, torn

1 tsp finely chopped ginger

1 tsp thyme leaves, plus extra
for garnish (optional)

1 tsp ground cumin

1 tsp ground allspice

1 tsp smoked paprika

Black pepper, to taste

Roti (page 56), to serve

Whenever I return from my travels—whether it's a week or months on end—Mom makes me stewed chicken and roti. I have scrutinized the recipe, studying her methodology countless times, yet I can never replicate it to the same standard. The only reason this recipe even comes close is because she helped me write it. Thanks, Mom.

Heat oil in a saucepan over medium heat. Add garlic, tomatoes, onion, celery and Wiri Wiri chili pepper. Sauté for 5–6 minutes, or until onion is translucent.

Add chicken and the remaining ingredients. Increase heat to medium-high and sauté for 10–15 minutes, stirring frequently to prevent burning. When the moisture from the chicken dries out, pour in 2 cups warm water, cover and bring to a boil. Reduce heat to medium-low and simmer for 15–20 minutes, stirring occasionally.

Transfer to a serving platter and garnish with Wiri Wiri chili peppers and thyme (if using). Serve with roti.

NOTE: Wiri Wiri chili peppers can be substituted with half the amount of Scotch bonnet or habanero chili peppers.

GUYANESE CHICKEN CURRY

SERVES 4

MARINATED CHICKEN

2 sprigs thyme, leaves only

1 Wiri Wiri chili pepper, thinly sliced (see Note)

3 Tbsp curry powder

2 Tbsp garam masala

1½ Tbsp salt

1 tsp black pepper

2 tsp grapeseed or vegetable oil

4 lbs bone-in chicken pieces

CURRY

2 Tbsp grapeseed or vegetable oil

2 onions, finely chopped

10 cloves garlic, finely chopped

5 sprigs thyme, leaves only

2 Wiri Wiri chili peppers, thinly sliced (see Note)

¼ cup curry powder

3 Tbsp garam masala

1 Tbsp ground cumin

2 Tbsp Green Seasoning (page 167)

2 tsp salt, plus extra to taste

Cilantro leaves, for garnish

Mom's Dhal (page 79), to serve

Steamed rice or Roti (page 56), to serve

Arguably Guyana's most recognizable dish, a good chicken curry has the same wholesome attributes as a soulful bowl of chicken noodle soup—all at once, it's recognizable, nostalgic, comforting and satiating.

MARINATED CHICKEN In a large bowl, combine all ingredients, except chicken. Add chicken and mix well. Allow to marinate in the fridge for at least 1 hour, or preferably overnight.

CURRY Heat oil in a large Dutch oven over medium heat. Add onions and sauté for 3–4 minutes, until lightly golden brown. Add garlic and sauté for 2 minutes. Combine remaining ingredients, except cilantro, in a bowl with ¼ cup water and mix well. Add mixture to the pan, then reduce heat to medium-low. Sauté for 10–15 minutes, scraping the bottom to prevent anything from burning. Add a splash of water if the mixture becomes too dry.

Add marinated chicken, mix well and cover. Cook for 25–30 minutes, stirring occasionally, until the water from the chicken has reduced, then add 1–2 cups water, depending on how much gravy is desired. Cover, then simmer for 20–25 minutes. Season to taste with salt.

Garnish with cilantro and serve with dhal and rice or roti.

NOTE: Wiri Wiri chili peppers can be substituted with half the amount of Scotch bonnet or habanero chili peppers.

BOMBAY TOMATO CHICKEN PARMIGIANA
WITH ARUGULA-WALNUT PESTO

SERVES 4

BOMBAY TOMATO SAUCE
2 cups tomato purée (passata)

2 tsp fenugreek leaves

1 tsp salt

1 tsp sugar

1 tsp ground turmeric

1 tsp red chili powder

1 tsp ground coriander

1 tsp amchur powder

½ tsp ground cumin

½ tsp onion powder

½ tsp garlic powder

1 tsp fresh lemon juice

CHICKEN PARMIGIANA
4 boneless, skinless chicken thighs

1 cup flour

2 eggs, beaten

1 cup panko breadcrumbs

Salt and black pepper, to taste

1 Tbsp vegetable oil

150 g (5½ oz) buffalo mozzarella, sliced into ⅓-inch pieces

½ cup grated Parmigiano-Reggiano, plus extra for garnish

ARUGULA-WALNUT PESTO
1 cup packed arugula leaves

1 cup packed basil leaves

½ cup walnuts

¾ cup grated Parmigiano-Reggiano

½ cup extra-virgin olive oil

1 Tbsp fresh lemon juice

3 cloves garlic

½ tsp salt

¼ tsp black pepper

This dish has been heavily inspired by one of my favorite dishes in the world, chicken parm. Crispy chicken smothered in a rich, spice-infused tomato sauce and melted cheese ... what's not to love?

BOMBAY TOMATO SAUCE In a medium saucepan, combine all ingredients and simmer over medium heat for 20 minutes. Set aside until required.

CHICKEN PARMIGIANA Place a chicken thigh in a freezer bag or cover it with plastic wrap on a cutting board. Using a mallet or rolling pin, gently flatten it to a ¼-inch thickness. (This helps for quick and even cooking.) Repeat with the remaining thighs.

Place flour, eggs and panko in 3 separate dishes. Season each with salt and pepper. Dredge chicken in the flour, shaking off the excess. Dip chicken into the beaten egg, then allow excess to drip off. Finally, press both sides of chicken into the panko. Place on a large plate. Repeat with the remaining thighs. Set aside.

Preheat oven to 430°F.

Heat oil in a large cast-iron or heavy-bottomed ovenproof pan over medium-high heat. Add chicken and sear for 5–6 minutes on each side, until golden brown. Transfer to a wire rack or a plate. Wipe the pan of crumbs, then return the chicken to the pan off the heat.

Top each chicken thigh with a ladle of sauce, mozzarella and Parmigiano-Reggiano. Bake for 6–8 minutes until the chicken is cooked through and the internal temperature reaches 165°F. Remove the pan from the oven.

ARUGULA-WALNUT PESTO Meanwhile, combine all the ingredients in a blender and blend to a grainy consistency. (This is not a purée–you do not want it smooth!) Set aside.

ASSEMBLY Set the oven to broil, then return the pan to the oven and broil for 1–2 minutes, until the cheese is golden brown and bubbly. You'll want to keep an eye on the pan as it happens quickly. Set aside to rest for 2–3 minutes.

Transfer to a serving platter or individual plates, top with Parmigiano-Reggiano and serve with arugula-walnut pesto.

SPICY JAMAICAN BEEF PATTY

MAKES 5

PASTRY
2 cups flour
1 tsp baking powder
2 tsp curry powder
1 tsp ground turmeric
2 Tbsp vegetable shortening, chilled
2 Tbsp butter, chilled
1 tsp salt

FILLING
2 tsp vegetable oil
2 lbs ground beef
2–3 Scotch bonnet chili peppers,
to taste, chopped
3 scallions, chopped
1½ tsp salt
1 tsp paprika
¾ tsp cayenne
1¼ tsp ground allspice
1 tsp thyme leaves
1 tsp garlic powder
¾ tsp onion powder
¾ tsp garam masala
¼ cup beef stock or water
2 tsp browning sauce (see Note)
2 tsp soy sauce

ASSEMBLY
1 egg, beaten
¼ cup (½ stick) butter, chilled

A succulent and spicy beef filling enveloped in a tidy little parcel of flaky pastry… the Jamaican beef patty is one of the best snacks ever. They've been a part of my life since childhood; their ubiquitous presence at family and community gatherings has always been a reliable source of comfort.

PASTRY In the bowl of a stand mixer fitted with a hook attachment, combine all ingredients. Working quickly to prevent butter from melting, process until the mixture forms pea-sized crumbs.

Pour in ½ cup ice-cold water and mix until a ball of dough has formed. Flatten into a disk, wrap in plastic wrap and chill in the fridge until needed.

FILLING Heat oil in a large frying pan over medium heat. Add beef and sear for 3 minutes. Add the remaining ingredients and simmer for 7–8 minutes, until stock has reduced by half. Using an immersion blender, pulse the beef mixture several times. Transfer filling to a baking sheet and spread out evenly to cool. Set aside.

ASSEMBLY Preheat oven to 400°F. Line a baking sheet with parchment paper.

In a small bowl, combine egg and 2 tsp water.

Remove pastry from fridge. Using a rolling pin, roll out dough to a large rectangle, about ⅛ inch thick.

Using a box grater, grate the cold butter over the dough. Fold it onto itself several times to form a square. Roll out dough again, about ⅛ inch thick.

Using a side plate as your template, trace out circles into the dough with a paring knife. Carefully spoon the cooled beef filling on one half of each disk. Brush edges with egg wash, then fold dough over to create a half moon. Using a fork, gently crimp the edges together. Brush tops with egg wash and place on the prepared baking sheet.

Bake for 25 minutes, until golden. Serve immediately.

NOTE: You'll find Jamaican browning sauce used everywhere throughout the Caribbean. Sugar is caramelized until deep and golden, then thinned out with water. You can buy it online or at West Indies supermarkets.

THE DESI CHEESE-BURGER

SERVES 4

TANDOORI-SPICED ONIONS

2 tsp butter

1 Tbsp Tandoori Masala (page 168)

2 large sweet onions, thinly sliced

¼ tsp salt

BURGER

½ cup store-bought or homemade Mayonnaise (page 50)

2 tsp chaat masala

2 lbs lean ground beef

½ tsp ground cumin

¾ tsp ground coriander

¾ tsp Kashmiri chili powder

1 tsp garlic powder

1½ tsp salt

¾ tsp black pepper

Cooking spray

4 slices American Cheddar

ASSEMBLY

4 hamburger buns

2 Tbsp Green Chutney (page 176)

4 butter lettuce leaves

1 tomato, sliced

Salt and black pepper, to taste

French fries, to serve

In my book, every season is BBQ season. While you could technically cook your burger in a frying pan, you won't get the same delicious, char-grilled intensity as you will from a grill. If you've not done so already, it's time to invest in a BBQ and level up your grill game!

TANDOORI-SPICED ONIONS Melt butter in a large frying pan over medium heat. Add tandoori masala and mix for 30–45 seconds. Add onions and salt and sauté for 10 minutes, until translucent and golden brown. Reduce heat to low and simmer for 10–15 minutes, until flavors are incorporated and onions are caramelized. Set aside.

BURGER Preheat a grill pan or BBQ to medium-high.

In a small bowl, combine mayo and chaat masala. Mix well and set aside.

In a medium bowl, combine beef with cumin, coriander, chili powder and garlic powder. Divide meat into 4 patties, each ¾ inch thick. With your finger, make a small indentation in the center of each patty to allow for a more even cook. Season both sides with salt and pepper.

Spray the grill with cooking spray. Add patties, cover and cook for 3–4 minutes, until golden. Flip, cover and cook for another 2–3 minutes. Flip again, top with cheese and cover until cheese has melted. Transfer patties to a large plate.

ASSEMBLY Spread a thin layer of chaat masala mayo on the cut side of each bun. Add ½ Tbsp of green chutney to each bottom bun. Top with lettuce and a slice of tomato and add patties. Season with salt and pepper. Add caramelized onions and top bun. Serve with fries and enjoy!

SPICY BEEF BOLOGNESE SAUCE

SERVES 6

2 Tbsp olive oil

1 Tbsp butter

4 cloves garlic, finely chopped

1 onion, finely chopped

1 stalk celery, finely chopped

1 small carrot, finely chopped

2 lbs ground beef

¾ cup white wine

1½ Tbsp tomato paste

2 cups chicken stock

2 tsp chili flakes

2 Wiri Wiri chili peppers, thinly sliced (see Note)

1 tsp dried oregano

½ cup 2% milk

½ cup torn basil leaves

Salt and black pepper, to taste

This versatile sauce was an instant hit when I released a version of it on my Instagram series Chef Dev at Home. Nearly all the ingredients are pantry staples, so it can be the basis of a delicious meal when I'm craving comfort food but too lazy to go to the grocery store.

The recipe can be easily doubled (or tripled) if you want to make a larger batch. Freeze the sauce in individual freezer bags and defrost it when you need dinner in a pinch— you can top pastas with it, use it as a filling for tacos or grilled cheeses, stuff it in peppers. See what I mean about versatility?

Heat oil and butter in a large cast-iron frying pan over medium heat. Add garlic, onion, celery and carrot and sauté for 7 minutes, until onion is softened and translucent. Move your vegetables to one side of the pan.

Add ground beef, using a wooden spoon to break it up. Cook for 5 minutes. Pour in wine and cook for another 5 minutes, or until alcohol is burned off and wine is completely reduced. Stir in tomato paste and sauté for 1–2 minutes.

Pour in stock. Add chili flakes, Wiri Wiri chili peppers and oregano. Bring to a boil, then reduce heat to a simmer. Partially cover and simmer for 1 hour, stirring occasionally.

Add milk and basil and simmer for another 30 minutes. Season to taste with salt and black pepper.

NOTE: Wiri Wiri chili peppers can be substituted with half the amount of Scotch bonnet or habanero chili peppers.

TANDOORI STEAK
WITH CHIMICHURRI

SERVES 2

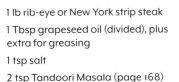

1 lb rib-eye or New York strip steak

1 Tbsp grapeseed oil (divided), plus extra for greasing

1 tsp salt

2 tsp Tandoori Masala (page 168)

1 Tbsp butter

1 tsp Ginger-Garlic Paste (page 167)

Chimichurri (page 178) or Roasted Red Pepper Chimichurri (page 178), to serve

Rich and aromatic, tandoori masala can add color and vibrancy to a savory dish. I use it as a flavorsome seasoning for rib-eye steak. If you prefer to grill the steak on the BBQ, you can melt the butter, tandoori masala and ginger-garlic paste together and use a brush to baste it on.

Set steak aside at room temperature for 1 hour. Preheat a cast-iron pan over medium-high heat.

Pat steak dry, then rub with 1 tsp oil. Evenly sprinkle salt over both sides.

Add the remaining 2 tsp oil to the pan and tilt to coat the bottom. Add steak and sear for 1 minute, then flip. Sear for another minute, then flip. Repeat until the internal temperature of the steak reaches 110°F.

Reduce heat to low, then add tandoori masala, butter and ginger-garlic paste to the pan. Using a spoon, baste steak with the melted butter. Cook for another 1–2 minutes, until the internal temperature of the steak reaches 125°F for medium-rare (or see chart below for your preferred doneness). Transfer steak to a cutting board and set aside to rest for 3 minutes. Flip, then rest for another 3 minutes.

Slice steak into ½-inch pieces on the diagonal. Transfer to a serving plate and serve with your preferred chimichurri.

Steak Temperatures

DONENESS	TEMPERATURE WHEN REMOVED FROM HEAT	FINAL COOKED TEMPERATURE
Rare	118°F	120°F
Medium-rare	125°F	130°F
Medium	136°F	140°F
Medium-well	143°F	148°F
Well done	154°F	160°F

PEPPERPOT

SERVES 4–6

2 Tbsp vegetable oil

3 lbs beef, lamb, goat or mutton chunks, washed

2 lbs oxtail

2 onions, chopped

5 sprigs thyme, plus extra for garnish

2 cinnamon sticks

2 (3-inch) dried orange peels

2 Tbsp salt

⅔ cup brown sugar

1 tsp whole cloves

2–3 Wiri Wiri chili peppers, chopped, to taste (see Note)

7 cloves garlic, finely chopped

1 Tbsp chopped ginger

1 cup cassareep

Guyanese Plait Bread (page 63), to serve

Guyana's national dish takes pride of place in my heart—after all, pepperpot is a treasured expression of my community, my heritage and my family, and something that I have enjoyed eating my entire life. I have fond memories of our Christmas trips to Guyana and taking in the enticing aromas of cassareep, cinnamon, cloves and orange peel in the air.

A good pepperpot starts with a high-quality cassareep (see "Cassareep" on page 128). Once cooked, the dish will rest overnight for the flavors to mingle. (Trust me, it will taste infinitely better.) Prepare it in advance, serve it with plait bread and there you have it, my friends—Guyana on a plate.

Heat oil in a large saucepan over medium-high heat. Add meat (in batches if necessary) and sear for 7–10 minutes, until brown on all sides. Transfer to a plate. Add oxtail to the pan and brown for 7–10 minutes. Transfer to the same plate.

To the pan, add onions, thyme, cinnamon, orange peels, salt, brown sugar, cloves and Wiri Wiri chili peppers. Sauté for 7–8 minutes, until onion is golden brown. Add garlic and ginger and sauté for 1 minute. Pour in 1 cup hot water, scraping the bottom of the pan to remove all the brown bits known as fond. (Don't neglect this step! It'll add flavor to the dish.)

Add the seared meat and oxtail back to the pan. Pour in cassareep and sauté for 4–5 minutes. Pour in 5 cups hot water and bring to a gentle boil, then reduce heat to medium-low and cover.

Simmer for 3–4 hours, until meat is tender. Set aside to rest overnight at room temperature.

As the cassareep helps to preserve the meat, the pepperpot can be kept at room temperature and reheated once a day for up to a week. Simply bring it to a boil until it's warmed through. (Alternatively, it can be refrigerated for up to 2 weeks.) Garnish with thyme and serve with plait bread.

NOTE: Wiri Wiri chili peppers can be substituted with half the amount of Scotch bonnet or habanero chili peppers.

CASSAREEP

When I was a child, we would often spend Christmas in Guyana. And it is on this festive occasion that most households will feast on Pepperpot (page 127). Its intoxicating aroma wafted across the homes of friends and families and through the streets.

The key ingredient in pepperpot is cassareep, a highly viscous and dark cassava-based liquid that lends a distinct color and bittersweet flavor while acting as a preservative. In my house, pepperpot is left on the stove for up to a week and reheated once a day (if it ever lasts that long!).

Amerindian Guyanese make cassareep by grating bitter cassava (page 85), then pressing it to extract the juice. (It is important to never drink that extracted cassava juice without boiling it first. When consumed in its raw state and combined with digestive enzymes, it produces cyanide and can be fatal.) The juice is then spiced with cinnamon, brown sugar and cloves and cooked for an extended time until thick and syrupy. Overall, it is an arduous process—cassava has such little water content so a lot of it is required to make even a decent amount.

Cassareep is mainly used to prepare pepperpot, and I have found great joy in replacing maple syrup with cassareep for pancakes, waffles and desserts. I also add it to salad dressings and sauces.

LAMB CURRY

SERVES 4–6

MARINATED LAMB
2 lbs lamb shoulder, cut into
2-inch pieces

1 Tbsp Green Seasoning (page 167)

2 Tbsp curry powder

1 Tbsp garam masala

2 tsp grapeseed oil

1½ tsp salt

CURRY
2 tsp grapeseed oil

1 onion, finely chopped

1 tsp salt

2 Wiri Wiri chili peppers, chopped
(see Note)

1 large cinnamon stick

1 star anise

2 Tbsp Ginger-Garlic Paste (page 167)

2 Tbsp curry powder

2 Tbsp Green Seasoning (page 167)

1 Tbsp garam masala

1 tsp ground cumin

2 potatoes, cut into 2-inch cubes

Steamed rice, to serve

MARINATED LAMB In a large bowl, combine all ingredients and mix well. Allow to marinate in the fridge for at least 2 hours, but preferably overnight.

CURRY Heat oil in a Dutch oven over medium heat. Add onion and salt and sauté for 5–6 minutes, until golden brown. Add Wiri Wiri chili peppers, cinnamon and star anise. Stir in ginger-garlic paste, curry powder, green seasoning, garam masala and cumin. Pour in ¼ cup water and stir. Cook for 2–3 minutes, stirring frequently, then add in lamb.

Cook for another 20 minutes, until the liquid has reduced and thickened. Add enough hot water to cover the meat. Reduce the heat to medium-low and partially cover. Braise for 1 hour, until meat is almost tender. Add potatoes and cook for another 15–20 minutes, until tender.

Serve with steamed rice.

NOTE: Wiri Wiri chili peppers can be substituted with half the amount of Scotch bonnet or habanero chili peppers.

LAMB VINDALOO MEATBALLS

SERVES 4

MEATBALLS

2 slices white bread, crust removed

3 Tbsp 2% milk

2 lbs ground lamb

1 egg

2 Tbsp finely chopped parsley

2 Tbsp finely chopped cilantro

¼ cup grated Parmigiano-Reggiano, plus extra shaved for garnish

2 tsp salt

½ tsp black pepper

1 tsp chili flakes

Grapeseed oil, for searing

VINDALOO SAUCE

2 tsp grapeseed oil

1 onion, finely chopped

2 tsp salt, plus extra to taste

2 Tbsp Ginger-Garlic Paste (page 167)

¾ tsp ground cardamom

¾ tsp ground cloves

1 (2-inch) cinnamon stick

1 Tbsp ground coriander

1 tsp cumin seeds

½ tsp black mustard seeds

4 Thai green chili peppers, plus extra sliced for garnish

2 cups tomato purée (passata)

¼ cup white vinegar

¾ tsp sugar

Cooked spaghetti or another favorite starch, to serve (optional)

Torn basil leaves, for garnish

This is straight up, stick-to-the ribs comfort food that speaks to two of my food obsessions: meatballs and lamb vindaloo. When I was a kid, my first experience with vindaloo was an acidic and fiery slap in the face. These days, I seek it out every time I'm in India, and Goa in particular.

Here, I have classic meatballs swimming in a tantalizing pool of vindaloo sauce. It's best served with pasta—any type you prefer—yet it is versatile enough to accompany a bowl of steamed rice or a heaping side of mash.

MEATBALLS In a shallow bowl combine bread and milk. Set aside until milk is absorbed.

In a large bowl, combine soaked bread and the remaining ingredients, except oil. Mix well with your hands.

Line a baking sheet with parchment paper. Shape the mixture into meatballs, about 2 inches in diameter, and place on the prepared baking sheet.

Heat oil in a large Dutch oven over medium heat. Add meatballs and sear for 7–10 minutes, until golden brown on all sides. Work in batches, if necessary, to avoid overcrowding. Transfer back to the baking sheet and set aside.

VINDALOO SAUCE Heat oil in the Dutch oven. Add onion and salt and sauté over medium heat for 6–8 minutes until golden brown. Reduce heat to medium-low. Add ginger-garlic paste, spices and chili peppers and sauté for 5–6 minutes, until fragrant.

Stir in tomato purée, vinegar, sugar and ½ cup water. Reduce heat to low and simmer for 10–15 minutes. Using an immersion blender, blend until smooth. (Alternatively, use a blender.)

Season sauce to taste with salt. Add meatballs and simmer for another 15–20 minutes to meld the flavors.

Serve as is or with your choice of a starch. You can garnish with sliced Thai green chili peppers, torn basil leaves, and shaved Parmigiano-Reggiano. Chef's kiss!

SMOKED GOAT BIRYANI

SERVES 4–6

GOAT

2 lbs goat shoulder, cut into bite-sized pieces

2 Thai green chili peppers, finely chopped

2 Tbsp Ginger-Garlic Paste (page 167)

1 Tbsp salt

2 tsp Kashmiri chili powder

2 tsp dried fenugreek leaves (*kasoori methi*)

1½ tsp ground turmeric

1 tsp garam masala

¾ tsp ground cumin

¾ tsp ground coriander

¾ tsp ground nutmeg

½ tsp sugar

¾ cup plain yogurt

2 Tbsp grapeseed oil

1 Tbsp fresh lemon juice

Hickory chips, for smoking

CARAMELIZED ONIONS

2 Tbsp ghee

2 white onions, thinly sliced

¾ tsp salt

SAFFRON INFUSION

¼ cup warm milk

½ tsp saffron

This is the perfect advanced recipe to prepare when you want to up your cooking game. Making biryani requires time, patience and a bit of technical prowess: each grain of rice must be separated and infused with aromatics. And once you get this dish right—brace yourself—it's like winning the lottery. It makes an impressive showstopper to serve guests on a special occasion.

You'll need a smoking gun for this recipe.

GOAT Combine all ingredients, except hickory chips, in a large bowl. Mix and gently massage the marinade into the meat. Cover the bowl with plastic wrap, then use a paring knife to make a small incision in the surface of the plastic wrap.

Turn on the smoking gun and load the chamber with hickory chips. Once it begins to smoke, insert the tube end into the bowl, through the incision. Leave in until all the chips have been used and the bowl is cloudy. Remove gun, block the incision with another small piece of plastic wrap and allow to smoke for 5 minutes. Remove the plastic wrap to release the smoke. Cover the bowl and allow to marinate in the fridge for at least 2 hours, but preferably overnight.

CARAMELIZED ONIONS Heat ghee in a large saucepan over medium heat. Add onions and salt and sauté for 15–20 minutes, until deep brown and caramelized. Reduce heat if necessary to prevent them from burning.

SAFFRON INFUSION Warm milk in a small saucepan over medium heat, until it begins to steam. Stir in saffron, then set aside.

GRAVY Heat ghee in a Dutch oven over medium heat. Add onions and salt and sauté for 6–7 minutes, until golden brown. Add ginger-garlic paste and sauté for 2 minutes. Add spices and stir for 1–2 minutes, until fragrant. Add chili peppers and tomatoes and sauté for 3 minutes. Season to taste with salt.

Add marinated goat meat to the gravy and stir to combine. Sauté for 8–10 minutes, until the meat releases its natural juices and sauce has reduced and thickened. Pour in 1 cup boiling water and stir, scraping up any bits stuck to the bottom. (Known as fond, these bits are LOADED with flavor.) Bring to a boil, then reduce heat to medium-low and simmer, partially covered, for 45 minutes, or until the meat is tender. Remove from heat and set aside.

RICE Meanwhile, bring a large saucepan of water to a boil. Add ghee, lemon juice, salt and whole spices and bring back to a boil. Drain rice, then add it to the pan. Boil, uncovered, for precisely 9 minutes. Drain rice. Line a baking sheet with parchment paper. Spread rice out evenly to cool.

ASSEMBLY Preheat oven to 375°F.

Ensure that the goat curry is not dry—if it is, add ¾ cup boiling water and stir well. Top with a third of each of the mint, cilantro and caramelized onions. Cover with half the rice and repeat the process, then top with remaining rice. Drizzle with saffron milk. Scatter with remaining mint, cilantro and onions and top with lemon slices, or reserve for garnish after baking.

In a large bowl, combine flour and ¾ cup water and mix well. Knead to form a dough. Roll into a long, skinny rope. Cover the dish with the lid, then use the dough to seal the edge and trap the steam. (Alternatively, cover the top of the lid with foil.) Return the Dutch oven to the stove and heat on high for 4–5 minutes to get the heat back into the pan, then bake for 15 minutes.

Garnish with lemon slices, the remaining mint, cilantro and onions (if reserved before baking), and chili peppers. Serve with raita.

GRAVY

2 Tbsp ghee

2 onions, thinly sliced

2 tsp salt, plus extra to taste

3 Tbsp Ginger-Garlic Paste (page 167)

4 star anise

3 bay leaves

2 cinnamon sticks

2 tsp Kashmiri chili powder

2 tsp garam masala

1½ tsp ground coriander

1½ tsp ground turmeric

1 tsp ground cumin

1 tsp ground cardamom

5 Thai green chili peppers, finely chopped

2 tomatoes, finely chopped

RICE

1 Tbsp ghee

1 Tbsp fresh lemon juice

2 tsp salt

1 cinnamon stick

1 star anise

5 cloves

2 bay leaves

3 green cardamom pods

1 black cardamom pod

2 cups basmati rice, well rinsed and soaked for 30 minutes

ASSEMBLY

¼ cup chopped mint (divided)

½ cup chopped cilantro (divided)

1 lemon, sliced

1½ cups flour

Whole Thai green chili peppers, for garnish

Raita, to serve

Break off the
crust seal

Garnish with
lemon slices

Add fresh,
chopped herbs

Dig deep
to serve

Showstopping
Smoked Goat Biryani
(PG.132)

HOT, HOT,

PEPPER SAUCE

When I was growing up, Mom would always cook with intense, fiery heat. And if it dialed up the heat, she likely had it in her pantry: Wiri Wiri chili peppers, Scotch bonnets, habaneros, Thai bird's eye chili peppers, jalapenos, the list goes on.

Hot pepper sauce was a staple table condiment when I was growing up. It helps to whet the appetite, stimulate the senses, perk up otherwise bland foods and intensify most savory dishes.

My favorite hot sauces start with a foundation of Fermented Hot Peppers (page 139), then I build it up with more ingredients to add layers of sweetness, saltiness, sharpness and umami.

HEAT

Asian Pear
+ Gochujang

Passion Fruit
+ Honey

Peach +
Ginger +
Lemongrass

Date +
Tamarind

Mango +
Garlic +
Maple

FERMENTED HOT PEPPER SAUCE

MAKES 1 LITER

FERMENTED HOT PEPPERS
1 lb mixed chili peppers (I like Wiri Wiris, Scotch bonnets and habaneros), washed and stemmed
6¼ tsp salt
5 cups distilled water
½ onion, roughly chopped
½ cup garlic cloves

For all of you who enjoy hot sauce as much as I do, you need to try fermenting your peppers! Healthy probiotics are formed during the fermentation process and continue to form when the sauce is stored in the fridge. The result? A delicious condiment to add to your favorite dishes—with a flavor profile that only improves with age. And check out how the fermented hot peppers can be used as a foundation for some of my other favorite hot sauces on the next page.

FERMENTED HOT PEPPERS Cut peppers in half. This helps them break down faster. Add salt to the distilled water so it dissolves to create a brine.

In a sterilized 2-quart jar, combine hot peppers, onion and garlic. Add brine until peppers are fully covered.

Fill a small zip-top bag with some water. Place the bag in the jar to help submerge floating peppers. Loosely screw the lid onto the jar and store in a cool dry place. (Set jar in a small dish in case there are any leaks during the fermenting process.) Open the jar every 2–3 days to release any gas. Ferment for at least 2 weeks, or preferably 3 months.

Once fermented, these peppers can be used as the basis for a variety of hot sauces (see page 140).

FERMENTED HOT PEPPER SAUCE Transfer hot peppers, onions, garlic and 1 cup brine to a blender and blend until smooth.

Fermented hot pepper sauce can be stored in an airtight container in the fridge for up to a year after it has fermented. You could also transfer the hot sauce to a squeeze bottle with the tip uncovered, which would help it slowly ferment even more. Shake before using.

HIGH-VOLTAGE HOT SAUCES

I love these sauces because they serve my palate, but they're also designed to inspire—so please experiment with ingredients and create your own. The key is to have fun and make new discoveries. And if you come up with something good, please share your results! Some of the greatest things about our food community is our love of sharing and our sense of community and all the opportunities we have to learn from one another.

All of these hot sauces can be stored in airtight containers in the fridge for up to 1 year.

MANGO + GARLIC + MAPLE

MAKES 6 CUPS

1 cup Fermented Hot Peppers (page 139)

1 cup onion, diced

6 cloves garlic

¼ cup Garlic Confit (page 179)

1–2 red bell peppers, seeded, deveined and chopped (1 cup)

1 carrot, grated (1 cup)

1 cup mango pulp (I like the Alphonso variety)

1 Tbsp salt

⅛ tsp xanthan gum (optional)

½ cup water

½ cup maple syrup

2 Tbsp white vinegar

¼ cup apple cider vinegar

DATE + TAMARIND

MAKES 3 CUPS

5 cloves garlic
1 cup Fermented Hot Peppers (page 139)
1 cup dates, pitted, softened in
hot water and drained
¼ cup water
½ cup tamarind sauce
¼ cup apple cider vinegar
2 Tbsp white vinegar
2 tsp salt

ASIAN PEAR + GOCHUJANG

MAKES 2¼ CUPS

5 cloves garlic
1 Asian pear, cored
1 cup Fermented Hot Peppers (page 139)
½ cup gochujang (Korean chili paste)
2 Tbsp white vinegar
¼ cup apple cider vinegar
3 Tbsp brown sugar
2 tsp salt
⅛ tsp xanthan gum (optional)

PEACH + GINGER + LEMONGRASS

MAKES 4 CUPS

2 cups drained canned peaches
1 cup Fermented Hot Peppers (page 139)
¼ cup apple cider vinegar
2 Tbsp white vinegar
3 Tbsp finely chopped ginger
2 Tbsp finely chopped lemongrass
2 Tbsp brown sugar
1 Tbsp salt
⅛ tsp xanthan gum (optional)

PASSION FRUIT + HONEY

MAKES 2½ CUPS

5 cloves garlic
1 cup Fermented Hot Peppers (page 139)
1 cup passion fruit purée
3 Tbsp white vinegar
1 Tbsp apple cider vinegar
¼ cup honey
2 tsp salt
½ tsp ground turmeric
⅛ tsp xanthan gum (optional)

KEEP IT
CHILL

DRINKS & DESSERTS

GINGER BEER

My grandmother always used to make me ginger beer. The stronger it was, the more I loved it.

SERVES 12

1 lb ginger, peeled and grated
2 cinnamon sticks, plus extra for garnish
Peel of 1 orange
1 Tbsp whole cloves
2 cups sugar
¼ cup fresh lime juice
1½ tsp salt
Slices of crystallized ginger, for garnish

Bring 10 cups of water to a simmer in a large pot.

Add ginger, cinnamon, orange peel and cloves. Simmer for 5 minutes, then remove from heat. Add sugar, lime juice and salt, then set aside at room temperature for 24 hours. Strain and discard solids.

Enjoy over ice, garnished with a cinnamon stick and a slice of crystallized ginger, or as a mixer in a cocktail.

MANGO AND TAMARIND DARK 'N' STORMY

A Dark 'n' Stormy is a delicious cocktail made with ginger beer and dark rum (essentially, it's a Moscow Mule with rum instead of vodka). Skip the rum for an equally quenching mocktail.

SERVES 1

SIMPLE SYRUP
1 cup sugar

DARK 'N' STORMY
½ oz Simple Syrup (see here)
1 tsp tamarind purée
1 oz mango pulp
1 oz fresh lime juice
2 oz dark rum (optional)
4 oz Ginger Beer (page 144)
Lime wedge or lime peel twist, for garnish

SIMPLE SYRUP Combine sugar and ¾ cup water in a small saucepan over medium heat. Heat for 1–2 minutes, until sugar has completely dissolved. Pour into a container and set aside to cool.

DARK 'N' STORMY In a tall glass, combine simple syrup, tamarind purée, mango pulp and lime juice and stir well. Add ice, rum (if using) and ginger beer. Garnish with a lime wedge or lime peel twist and serve.

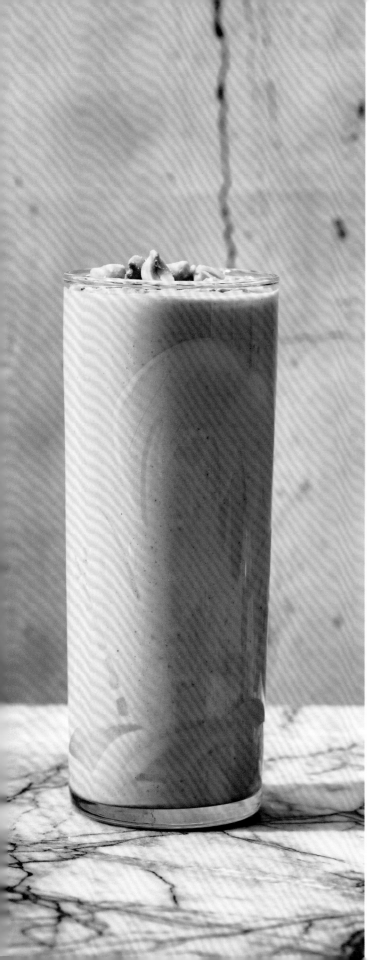

MANGO LASSI

SERVES 2

1½ cups chopped ripe mango or 1 cup mango pulp

1 cup plain yogurt

½ cup milk

1½ Tbsp honey

¼ tsp rose water (optional)

¼ tsp ground cardamom

¼ tsp ground cinnamon

½ tsp salt

½ cup ice

Pinch of saffron, for garnish (optional)

Combine all ingredients, except saffron, in a blender and blend for 2 minutes, until smooth.

Serve in chilled glasses. Garnish with a pinch of saffron (if using).

PEANUT PUNCH

SERVES 2

¾ cup peanuts

3 Tbsp peanut butter

1 cup coconut milk

¾ cup ice

1 banana

1½ Tbsp maple syrup

½ tsp vanilla extract

½ tsp ground cinnamon

¼ tsp ground nutmeg

¼ tsp ground cardamom

⅛ tsp ground ginger

Toasted peanuts, chopped, for garnish

Combine all ingredients in a blender and blend for 2 minutes, until smooth.

Serve in chilled glasses. Garnish with peanuts.

GARAM MASALA-SPICED PECAN PIE
WITH VANILLA ICE CREAM

SERVES 8

PIE CRUST

2½ cups flour, plus extra for dusting

½ cup vegetable shortening, cubed and chilled

11 Tbsp butter (1½ sticks less 1 Tbsp), grated from frozen

1 tsp ground cardamom

1 tsp salt

FILLING

1 cup packed dark brown sugar

1 tsp garam masala

¼ tsp ground cinnamon

¼ tsp ground cloves

1 tsp salt

¼ tsp ground nutmeg

3 eggs, beaten

1 cup light corn syrup

⅓ cup (⅔ stick) butter, melted

1½ tsp vanilla extract

ASSEMBLY

1½ cups pecans

Vanilla ice cream, to serve

This dessert delivers in every way. My cousin changed my world when she combined two of her favorite recipes together to create this baked perfection. One was for a pie crust; the other was for a pecan pie filling. It has everything that I want in a dessert: unctuous sweetness, buttery goodness, a flaky crust and a nutty finish. I enhance my version with warm garam masala spices, accentuating the earthy notes.

PIE CRUST Combine all ingredients in a food processor fitted with a blade attachment and process until it forms pea-sized crumbs. You'll want to work fast and keep the dough as cold as possible. (Alternatively, mix with your hands in a bowl.) Add ½ cup ice-cold water and mix until a dough ball forms. It should hold together and not be too sticky. Divide dough in half and pat down into 1-inch-thick disks. Wrap in plastic wrap and refrigerate for a minimum of 1 hour and up to 2 days.

FILLING In a bowl, combine brown sugar, garam masala, cinnamon, cloves, salt and nutmeg. Add eggs, corn syrup, butter and vanilla. Mix well, then set aside.

ASSEMBLY Preheat oven to 350°F.

Place a disk of dough on a work surface dusted with flour. (Save the second disk for another use; it can be frozen for up to 3 months.) Using a rolling pin, roll out dough, about 1 inch larger in diameter than your baking dish. (If dough is too sticky to work with, dust with a little more flour.) Roll up dough onto the rolling pin, then unroll over the pie dish. Gently press the dough into the edges and pinch and tuck the dough to form a clean crust.

Pour in filling, then evenly top with pecans. Loosely cover dish with aluminum foil and bake for 25 minutes. Remove foil, then bake for another 25 minutes, until set. Set aside to cool for at least 3 hours or overnight.

Slice, top with ice cream and serve.

FLOURLESS CHOCOLATE CAKE
WITH CARDAMOM GANACHE

SERVES 6–8

CHOCOLATE CAKE
½ cup (1 stick) butter, plus extra for greasing

1 cup chocolate chips

3 eggs

¾ cup sugar

½ cup unsweetened cocoa powder

¾ tsp salt

1 tsp ground espresso

½ tsp ground cinnamon

½ tsp Kashmiri chili powder

2 tsp vanilla extract

Smoked sea salt, for garnish (optional)

GANACHE
1 cup heavy (36%) cream

1 cup chocolate chips

½ tsp ground cardamom

½ tsp salt

CHOCOLATE CAKE Preheat oven to 375°F. Grease an 8-inch round cake pan, then line the bottom with parchment paper.

Bring a saucepan of water, about an inch deep, to a simmer over medium heat. Add chocolate chips and butter to a heatproof bowl and place over the saucepan. Stir occasionally, until chocolate has melted. Remove from heat.

Whisk eggs in a bowl. Add 2 Tbsp of melted chocolate and whisk in. (This technique, known as tempering, helps to bring the beaten eggs to the temperature of the chocolate without scrambling.) Add the egg mixture to the bowl and whisk. Stir in sugar.

Add cocoa, salt, espresso, cinnamon and chili powder. Stir in vanilla. Transfer batter to the prepared pan. Bake for 20–25 minutes, until a toothpick inserted into the center comes out clean. Set cake aside to cool.

GANACHE Heat cream gently in a small saucepan over medium heat, until it begins to steam and simmer.

In a stainless-steel bowl, combine chocolate chips, cardamom and salt. Pour in hot cream and stir until chocolate has melted.

ASSEMBLY Remove cake from pan and set on a wire rack. Pour ganache over the cake, then transfer to a plate and garnish with sea salt (if using). Slice and serve!

SPICED STRAWBERRYRHUBARB COBBLER

SERVES 6

SPICED STRAWBERRY-RHUBARB FILLING

2 Tbsp butter

4 cups strawberries, hulled and quartered

1–2 stalks rhubarb, cut into 1-inch pieces (2 cups)

3 Tbsp sugar

2 tsp lemon zest

¾ tsp ground cinnamon

¾ tsp ground allspice

¾ tsp ground nutmeg

½ tsp ground cardamom

¾ tsp salt

2 tsp vanilla extract

1 Tbsp cornstarch

CRUMBLE

½ cup all-purpose flour

½ cup rolled oats

¼ cup chopped walnuts

¼ cup packed brown sugar

¾ tsp baking powder

¾ tsp ground cardamom

1 tsp salt

½ cup (1 stick) butter, cubed and chilled

ASSEMBLY

Plain yogurt or ice cream, to serve

SPICED STRAWBERRY-RHUBARB FILLING Melt butter in a large saucepan over medium heat. Add remaining ingredients, except cornstarch, and sauté for 10–12 minutes. Stir in cornstarch, then remove from heat and set aside.

CRUMBLE In a mixing bowl, combine flour, oats, walnuts, sugar, baking powder, cardamom and salt. Mix well. Using your hands, mix the butter cubes into the mixture, until it forms pea-sized clumps. Place in the freezer for 15–20 minutes. (This helps to chill the butter before baking.)

ASSEMBLY Preheat oven to 375°F. Line a baking sheet with parchment paper.

Transfer filling to a 9-inch baking dish. Top evenly with the crumble. Place the baking dish on the prepared baking sheet. Bake for 35–45 minutes, until topping is golden brown and fruit mixture is bubbling. Set aside for 15 minutes.

Serve with plain yogurt (or ice cream).

ALLSPICE BROWNIES
WITH VANILLA GLAZE

SERVES 6–8

BROWNIES

½ cup (1 stick) butter, room temperature, plus extra for greasing

2½ cups semi-sweet chocolate chips (divided)

¾ cup sugar

¾ cup brown sugar

4 eggs

2 tsp vanilla extract

¾ tsp ground allspice

½ tsp ground cinnamon

½ tsp salt

1 cup flour

VANILLA GLAZE

1 cup confectioners' sugar

2 tsp vanilla extract

Moist, dense and gooey, this sweet treat has a crazy superpower when shared: it brings smiles to gatherings, bridges generational age gaps and makes friends out of foes. (True story.) Who can resist it?

Here is my twist on this beautiful classic. It's not like it needed any of my assistance, but I find that an addition of aromatic allspice adds a bit of warmth to build more layers of comforting flavor.

BROWNIES Preheat oven to 325°F. Grease a 9 × 13-inch baking pan, then line it with parchment paper.

Bring a saucepan of water, about an inch deep, to a simmer over medium heat. Add 2 cups chocolate chips and the butter to a heatproof bowl and place over the saucepan. Stir occasionally, until the chips are melted, then remove from heat and set aside.

Combine both sugars in a large bowl. Whisk in eggs, one at a time, until well incorporated.

Add vanilla, allspice, cinnamon and salt. Gently whisk in the chocolate mixture. Sift flour into the bowl, then fold in. Fold in the remaining ½ cup chocolate chips.

Pour the batter into the prepared baking pan and use a spatula to smooth out the top.

Bake for 25–30 minutes, until a toothpick inserted into the center comes out clean. Set aside to cool completely.

VANILLA GLAZE Meanwhile, combine sugar and vanilla in a bowl. Add 2 Tbsp plus 2 tsp water and whisk until smooth.

Top the cooled pan of brownies with vanilla glaze, then slice and serve.

CHOCOLATE CHIP COOKIES

MAKES 20

¾ cup packed brown sugar

½ cup sugar

½ cup (1 stick) butter, melted

1 egg, beaten

1 tsp vanilla extract

1¼ cups flour

1 tsp salt

½ tsp baking soda

1⅓ cups semi-sweet chocolate chips

This recipe was an instant classic when I featured it on my online series Chef Dev at Home. *During the pandemic, so many families were coming together in the kitchen to bake these treats. The video put smiles on everyone's faces— including my niece, Maia, who would watch the video at bedtime. It melted my heart.*

Knowing full well that not everyone has a stand mixer, I offered a recipe that could be prepared by hand.

In a bowl, combine both sugars and butter and mix well. Whisk in egg and vanilla.

Sift in flour, salt and baking soda. Stir in chocolate chips and combine to form a dough. Wrap dough in plastic wrap and refrigerate for 1 hour.

Preheat oven to 350°F. Line a baking sheet with parchment paper.

Remove dough from fridge and form dough balls, about 2 inches in diameter, and place on the prepared baking sheet, evenly spaced 2 inches apart. Bake for 8–10 minutes, until the edges are light brown and the center is soft.

SPICED CHALLAH BREAD PUDDING
WITH SALTED VANILLA CARAMEL

SERVES 6–8

SPICED CHALLAH BREAD PUDDING
Butter, for greasing
1 loaf day-old challah, cut into
1½-inch cubes
5 eggs
¾ cup packed brown sugar
2 tsp orange zest
1 tsp salt
¾ tsp ground cinnamon
¾ tsp ground cardamom
¾ tsp ground cloves
½ tsp ground nutmeg
4 cups whole milk

SALTED VANILLA CARAMEL
1 cup sugar
½ cup heavy (36%) cream
1 Tbsp butter
¾ tsp salt
1 tsp vanilla extract

SPICED CHALLAH BREAD PUDDING Preheat oven to 375°F.

Grease a large baking dish. Add challah.

Combine remaining ingredients in a large bowl and whisk well. Pour mixture over the bread and set aside for 10 minutes for challah to soak up the flavors.

Bake for 45 minutes, until a toothpick inserted into the center comes out clean. Set aside for 10–15 minutes to cool.

SALTED VANILLA CARAMEL Meanwhile, heat sugar in a large saucepan over medium-low heat, until sugar begins to melt around the edges. Gently fold, until it turns amber. Remove from heat.

Carefully stir in cream and butter. Add salt and vanilla. Set aside.

Drizzle bread pudding with salted vanilla caramel. Slice and serve.

SAFFRON KHEER

SERVES 4

¼ cup basmati rice

2 tsp ghee

4 green cardamom pods, crushed

1 cinnamon stick

4 cups whole milk

Pinch of saffron, plus extra for garnish

5 Tbsp sugar

3 Tbsp chopped nuts (such as cashews, almonds, pistachios), plus extra for garnish

2 Tbsp golden raisins

¼ tsp ground nutmeg

1 tsp rose water

Saffron kheer is a slow-cooked sweet rice pudding infused with fragrant spices and aromatics. Growing up, it was always a satisfying conclusion to a home-cooked meal, but it was also a comforting treat to be enjoyed on Sundays at temple. There, the kheer was served in Styrofoam cups, but its practical and modest serving style didn't detract from its taste—I always enjoyed it.

Rinse rice under cold running water, until water runs clear. Soak rice in a small bowl of room temperature water for 30 minutes.

In a heavy-bottomed saucepan, combine ghee, drained rice, cardamom and cinnamon. Toast over medium-low heat for 3–4 minutes, until fragrant.

Pour in milk and increase heat to medium. Bring to a gentle simmer, then stir in saffron and sugar.

Cook rice, uncovered, for 25–30 minutes, stirring continuously to prevent burning, until tender. Fold in nuts, raisins and nutmeg. Simmer for another 5 minutes to infuse flavors. Stir in rose water. Remove from heat.

Serve warm or chilled, garnished with nuts and saffron.

JALEBI

SERVES 6–8

BATTER
1 cup flour
¼ cup corn flour (see Note)
½ tsp salt
¼ tsp baking soda
¼ cup plain yogurt
5 drops organic orange food coloring

SYRUP
1½ cups sugar
¼ tsp ground cardamom
2 tsp fresh lemon juice
½ tsp saffron

ASSEMBLY
2 cups grapeseed oil, for frying
½ cup toasted pistachios, coarsely chopped, for garnish

As a child, I would enjoy this crispy Indian funnel cake at religious functions and on special occasions. It was so sweet, so flavorful and full of texture. My dear Auntie Yasmine would come over with a box of jalebi especially for me.

BATTER In a large bowl, combine flour, corn flour, salt and baking soda and whisk well. Add yogurt, food coloring and 150 mL water and whisk gently. The goal is to achieve a batter slightly runnier than pancake batter; if the batter is too thick, add ½ tsp water at a time to achieve desired consistency. Set aside for 20 minutes to rest.

SYRUP Meanwhile, combine all the syrup ingredients in a medium saucepan. Pour in ¾ cup water and bring to a boil. Boil for 3–4 minutes, then remove from heat.

ASSEMBLY Line a baking sheet with parchment paper.

Heat oil in a large saucepan over medium heat. Pour batter into a squeeze bottle. (If you don't have a squeeze bottle, pour it into a zip-top bag and make a small cut in the corner.)

Starting at the center, pour batter into the hot oil and spiral out, making 5–6 loops. Repeat with a couple more, ensuring they do not overlap. Fry for 1 minute, then flip over and fry for another minute.

Using a slotted spoon, transfer your jalebi to the warm syrup and soak for several seconds, then transfer to the prepared baking sheet. Garnish with pistachios. Repeat with the remaining batter. Set aside for 5–10 minutes, then serve.

Jalebis can be stored in an airtight container at room temperature for 5 days.

NOTE: Corn flour—not to be mistaken with cornstarch—is a smooth and fine flour milled from dried corn kernels. It tends to be yellow, but is also available in white or blue.

PARSAD

SERVES 6–8

½ cup (1 stick) salted butter
1 cup flour
1 cup 2% milk
1 cup evaporated milk
½ cup sugar
3 Tbsp raisins
⅓ tsp ground cardamom
¼ tsp ground cinnamon
¼ tsp ground nutmeg
¼ cup maraschino cherries, chopped

One of my favorite responsibilities as a child was to help distribute a pudding-like dessert known as parsad after Sunday service at temple. It is also known as mohan bhog, meaning "offering for the Lord."

Mom would always make ample batches of parsad for weddings and other functions for the community—the dish never failed her. She explained that the key to getting it right was all in the technique. She would first make a roux, then add enough milk to create a very thick béchamel.

Thanks for the recipe, Mom!

Melt butter in a large saucepan over medium heat. Stir in flour and cook out for 15–20 minutes, until nutty and deep golden brown. Reduce heat, if necessary, to prevent the roux from burning.

Meanwhile, in a separate saucepan, combine milk, evaporated milk, sugar, raisins, cardamom, cinnamon and nutmeg. Mix well and bring to a simmer over medium-low heat.

Gradually pour the milk mixture into the pan with the roux. Stir continuously, until smooth. Stir in cherries until the mixture pulls away from the sides and comes together.

Transfer to a serving bowl and serve warm.

RICOTTA RASMALAI

MAKES 12

RICOTTA PATTIES

Vegetable oil, for greasing

2 cups ricotta cheese, drained overnight

2 Tbsp milk powder

¼ cup sugar

½ tsp salt

¼ tsp ground cardamom

¼ tsp ground cinnamon

¼ tsp ground nutmeg

SWEETENED MILK (*RABDI*)

2½ cups whole milk

1 cup condensed milk

2 tsp rose water

¾ tsp ground cardamom

Pinch of saffron

ASSEMBLY

¼ cup toasted and finely chopped pistachios

¼ cup toasted and finely chopped almonds

⅓ tsp saffron

Few desserts excite me more than the Bengali rasmalai—it gives me all the feels. Silky smooth cheese patties, made with paneer or chenna, are soaked in a sweet, spiced milk. Here, I've simplified the recipe by preparing it with ricotta. Trust me, this is something to write home about.

RICOTTA PATTIES Preheat oven to 350°F. Grease two 12-cup muffin pans.

Combine the remaining ingredients in a bowl and mix until smooth. Add 2 Tbsp of the mixture to each muffin cup. Gently press down on each to form a patty, about ¾ inch thick. Bake for 35 minutes.

SWEETENED MILK (*RABDI*) Meanwhile, combine all the rabdi ingredients in a saucepan over medium-low heat and simmer for 6–7 minutes. Set aside to cool to room temperature.

ASSEMBLY Pour rabdi into a baking dish. (It should fill it halfway.) Add ricotta patties and coat in the sauce. Soak overnight and up to 2 days for best results. Garnish with toasted pistachios, toasted almonds and saffron.

SHRIKHAND CANNOLI

SERVES 6–8

MANGO SHRIKHAND

¾ cup Greek yogurt

1 cup mascarpone cheese

¼ cup mango pulp (I like the Alphonso variety)

½ cup confectioners' sugar

¾ tsp salt

½ tsp ground cardamom

½ tsp ground cinnamon

4 tsp ground nutmeg

Pinch of saffron

CANNOLI SHELLS

2 cups flour, plus extra for dusting and as needed

2½ Tbsp light brown sugar

⅓ tsp ground green cardamom

½ tsp salt

3 Tbsp cold butter

½ cup marsala or dry white wine

2 eggs

Vegetable oil, for frying

1 egg white, beaten

ASSEMBLY

½ cup toasted and chopped pistachios, for garnish

SPECIAL EQUIPMENT

Cannoli molds (see Note)

NOTE: Cannoli molds are used to make the pastry shells for the fillings. You can buy them at specialty kitchenware shops or online.

One of the best joys in life has to be cannoli—they are so much fun to eat and are loved by people of all ages.

They're also super versatile because they can be piped with any type of filling imaginable. Here, I've combined the shells with mango shrikhand, which could also be enjoyed on its own. Shrikhand is a thick and creamy East Indian dessert made traditionally with pressed yogurt, but I use plain Greek yogurt for ease. It's the perfect dessert for when cravings call for something quick and sweet.

MANGO SHRIKHAND In a large bowl, combine all ingredients. Fold together using a spatula. Refrigerate until needed.

CANNOLI SHELLS In a large bowl, combine flour, sugar, cardamom and salt and whisk to combine. Add butter and mix between your fingers until it forms pea-sized crumbs.

Mix in marsala (or wine) and the 2 eggs. Knead several times until a smooth dough ball forms. (Add more flour 1 tsp at a time if necessary.) Wrap in plastic wrap and refrigerate for at least 1 hour.

Heat oil in a deep fryer or large saucepan to a temperature of 350°F. Line a baking sheet with paper towels.

Divide the dough in half. Using a rolling pin, roll out the first piece of dough on a lightly floured work surface to a thickness of ⅛ inch. Using a 3-inch ring mold, punch out disks. Repeat with the remaining piece of dough.

Add 2 tsp water to the beaten egg white to create an egg wash. Lightly flour a cannoli mold and wrap a pastry disk around it, brushing the disk where it overlaps with egg wash and pressing down firmly to seal the tube. Repeat with the remaining molds and pastry disks.

Using tongs, carefully lower cannoli shells (around their molds) into the fryer or pan, taking care not to splash hot oil. (If necessary, work in batches to avoid overcrowding.) Fry for 3–4 minutes, until golden brown. Transfer to the prepared baking sheet to drain. Repeat with the remaining pastry dough. Allow shells to cool before removing from molds.

Use the corner of a dish towel to gently pull the cannoli shells off the molds.

ASSEMBLY Place chopped pistachios in a shallow bowl.

Fill a piping bag with shrikhand. (The colder this mixture is, the better it will hold; place in the freezer for 20 minutes to firm up if necessary.) Pipe the filling into the cannoli shells, then dip both ends in pistachios. Serve immediately.

BACK TO BASICS

PANTRY ESSENTIALS

Ginger-Soy
Glaze

Chipotle-
Cassareep
BBQ Sauce

Green
Seasoning

Ginger-Garlic
Paste

Tandoori
Masala

Jerk
Marinade

SEASONINGS & MARINADES

GINGER-GARLIC PASTE

Essential for cooking many South Asian recipes, this paste is a versatile flavor bomb that complements many savory dishes.

MAKES 1 CUP

¾ cup garlic cloves
½ cup roughly chopped ginger
2 Tbsp grapeseed oil

Combine all ingredients in a food processor. Add 3 Tbsp water and blend until smooth.

The ginger-garlic paste can be stored in an airtight container in the fridge for up to 3 weeks or in the freezer for up to 6 months.

GREEN SEASONING

This essential Caribbean seasoning adds herbaceous vibrancy to sauces, curries and stir fries, taking your food from good to out of this world.

MAKES 2 CUPS

2 Wiri Wiri chili peppers (see Note)
1 onion, chopped
⅓ cup garlic cloves
1 cup chopped tomato
1 (2-inch) piece ginger, chopped
½ cup chopped celery
2–3 scallions, chopped
¾ cup roughly chopped culantro (*chadon beni*)
¾ cup cilantro
1 cup roughly chopped parsley
2 tsp thyme leaves
2 tsp salt
2 tsp fresh lime juice
1 Tbsp oil

Combine all ingredients in a blender and blend to desired consistency.

Green seasoning can be stored in an airtight container in the fridge for up to a week.

NOTE: Wiri Wiri chili peppers can be substituted with half the amount of Scotch bonnet or habanero chili peppers.

GINGER-SOY GLAZE

A little goes a long way with this tasty condiment. Use it to jazz up rice dishes, sashimi, sushi and seafood dishes. It makes a great salad dressing, too. And because the recipe calls for gluten-free soy sauce, it can be used for dishes that need to meet that dietary requirement.

MAKES ¾ CUP

1 cup gluten-free soy sauce
½ cup honey
3 Tbsp rice vinegar
1 Tbsp sesame oil
1 Tbsp sugar
2 tsp minced ginger

Combine all ingredients in a saucepan. Simmer for 5–6 minutes over medium heat, until thickened. (Strain out ginger if you prefer.)

TANDOORI MASALA

This is my secret weapon spice blend—a versatile South Asian seasoning designed to elevate plain roasted veggies, seafood or meat proteins.

MAKES ¾ CUP

3 Tbsp dried fenugreek leaves (*kasoori methi*)
2½ Tbsp Kashmiri chili powder
1 Tbsp ground coriander
2 tsp ground cardamom
2 tsp ground ginger
2 tsp garlic powder
1½ tsp ground turmeric
2 tsp beetroot powder (see Note)
2 tsp salt
1½ tsp black pepper
1½ tsp ground cumin
¾ tsp ground cloves
½ tsp ground mace
¼ tsp ground nutmeg
½ tsp ground cinnamon

Combine all ingredients in an airtight container and shake to blend.

This tandoori seasoning can be stored in an airtight container in a cool dry place for up to 1 year.

NOTE: Beetroot powder is simply dried and ground beetroot. Loaded with vitamins and minerals, this high-fiber, low-fat ingredient has an intense beet flavor and color. You can buy it at specialty food shops or online.

CHIPOTLE-CASSAREEP BBQ SAUCE

While ubiquitous in a Guyanese Pepperpot (page 127), cassareep is rarely seen in the form of a condiment or dressing. Here, its earthy notes play off smoky chipotle. Every time I serve anything with cassareep, people take delight in its unique flavor.

This sauce is a versatile summer condiment. I pair it with BBQ wings, ribs and burgers. In fact, it can replace anything calling for BBQ sauce or ketchup. I mean, if that isn't versatile …

MAKES 5 CUPS

2 tsp grapeseed oil

1 onion, finely chopped

1 tsp salt

1 (7-fl oz) can chipotle peppers in adobo sauce

¾ cup packed brown sugar

1 tsp onion powder

1 tsp garlic powder

1 tsp chipotle chili powder

½ tsp ground cumin

½ tsp ground cinnamon

1½ cups tomato purée (passata)

½ cup ketchup

¾ cup apple cider vinegar

1¾ cups water

2 Wiri Wiri chili peppers, chopped (see Note)

½ cup cassareep

Heat oil in a saucepan over medium heat. Add onion and salt and sauté for 5–6 minutes, until golden brown. Add remaining ingredients and simmer for 20–25 minutes, stirring occasionally, until desired consistency is reached. (It should be thick and viscous.)

Remove from heat. Using an immersion blender, blend until smooth.

This BBQ sauce can be stored in an airtight container in the fridge for up to 2 weeks.

JERK MARINADE

I don't know what I'd do without this recipe. I use it to marinate meats but it's versatile enough to amplify vegetables, paneer and tofu. It's a flavor-forward recipe from Jamaica!

MAKES 1⅓ CUPS

10 cloves garlic

4 scallions, chopped

2–3 Scotch bonnet chili peppers, to taste

1 small onion, finely chopped

1 (2-inch) piece ginger, roughly chopped

2 Tbsp brown sugar

1 Tbsp thyme leaves

2 tsp ground allspice

¾ tsp ground cinnamon

½ tsp salt

½ tsp ground nutmeg

½ cup gluten-free soy sauce

2 Tbsp tamarind purée

1½ Tbsp fresh lime juice

Combine all ingredients in a blender and blend until smooth.

This marinade can be stored in the fridge for up to 2 weeks.

> Note: Wiri Wiri chili peppers can be substituted with half the amount of Scotch bonnet or habanero chili peppers.

Creamy
Feta
Dressing

Spicy Caesar
Dressing

Vegan
Hollandaise

Spicy Cheese
Sauce

Citrus
Vinaigrette

Cassareep
Dressing

DRESSINGS & SAUCES

CITRUS VINAIGRETTE

Often while cooking, it can become clear that a dish just needs an added burst of vibrancy or flavor. That is where this vinaigrette comes in— it will make your dishes pop!

MAKES 1¼ CUPS

¾ cup grapeseed oil

2 Tbsp + 1 tsp apple cider vinegar

5 Tbsp fresh lemon juice

¼ cup fresh orange juice

¼ cup fresh lime juice

¼ cup honey

1½ tsp salt

¾ tsp white pepper

¾ tsp granulated garlic

½ tsp onion powder

½ tsp ground cinnamon

1½ tsp Dijon mustard

Combine all ingredients in a blender and blend until emulsified. (Alternatively, whisk ingredients together in a bowl or shake in a jar.)

This vinaigrette can be stored in an airtight container in the fridge for up to 10 days.

SPICY CAESAR DRESSING

There is a reason the Caesar salad is one of the most popular in the world. These days, every home cook should have a dressing in their repertoire—and this one is a keeper. You can also toss it with pasta, pour it over potatoes or use it as a dip.

MAKES ABOUT ¾ CUP

3 cloves garlic, finely chopped

1 egg yolk

½ tsp red chili powder

2 Tbsp fresh lemon juice

1 Tbsp anchovy paste

2 tsp whole-grain Dijon mustard

2 tsp capers

1 tsp Worcestershire sauce

1 tsp Tabasco sauce

1 tsp lemon zest

¼ cup grated Parmigiano-Reggiano

Salt and black pepper, to taste

¼ cup + 1 Tbsp extra-virgin olive oil

Combine all ingredients, except oil, in a bowl. Add 2 tsp water and whisk. Slowly drizzle in oil, until emulsified. This dressing can be stored in the fridge for up to a week.

CASSAREEP DRESSING

I often see cassareep used in meat-based dishes, yet rarely in other applications. So I created this dressing! I want to expand the ways we use this incredible ingredient from Guyana.

MAKES ABOUT 1 CUP

⅓ cup grapeseed oil
¼ cup apple cider vinegar
¼ cup cassareep
1 tsp Dijon mustard
¼ cup brown sugar
¼ tsp ground cinnamon
1 Wiri Wiri chili pepper, finely chopped (see Note)
1½ tsp salt

Combine all ingredients in a blender and blend until smooth.

This dressing can be stored in an airtight container for a week.

> NOTE: Wiri Wiri chili peppers can be substituted with half the amount of Scotch bonnet or habanero chili peppers.

VEGAN HOLLANDAISE

If you love hollandaise sauce but prefer a healthier or dairy-free alternative, look no further. The cashews add lusciousness and creaminess to the sauce so it has the mouthfeel of a true hollandaise.

MAKES 1¾ CUPS

1 cup cashews, soaked for 1 hour in 1 cup hot water
¼ cup nutritional yeast
1½ tsp salt
1 tsp white pepper
1 tsp ground turmeric
½ tsp onion powder
¾ tsp garlic powder
1 Tbsp fresh lemon juice
1 tsp apple cider vinegar
1 tsp store-bought or homemade Hot Sauce (page 140)

Combine all ingredients in a blender, including the soaking water from the cashews, and blend until smooth. Pour into a saucepan and cook over low heat for 10 minutes, until reduced and thickened.

This hollandaise sauce can be stored in an airtight container in the fridge for up to a week.

SPICY CHEESE SAUCE

If I told you how many times I have made this cheese sauce, you probably would not believe me. I am glad I can share this variation with you and I encourage you to make it your own.

MAKES 4 CUPS

¼ cup (½ stick) butter

¼ cup flour

2 tsp store-bought or homemade Hot Sauce (page 140)

2 tsp garlic purée

1 tsp Dijon mustard

¾ tsp salt

¾ tsp cayenne

½ tsp ground turmeric

2¾ cups 2% milk

2 cups grated cheddar

1 cup grated mozzarella

½ cup grated Parmigiano-Reggiano

2 tsp fresh lemon juice

Melt butter in a saucepan over medium-low heat. Stir in flour and cook for 3 minutes, until it smells nutty. Stir in hot sauce, garlic purée, Dijon mustard, salt, cayenne and turmeric.

Slowly pour in the milk in three parts, mixing well and allowing it to thicken after each addition. Whisk in cheeses in three parts and whisk continuously until a thick sauce forms. (An immersion blender produces a very smooth consistency.)

Remove from heat, stir in lemon juice and enjoy. This sauce will keep in the fridge for up to a week. It also freezes well.

CREAMY FETA DRESSING

Feta has always been one of those cheeses with the power to make me weak in my knees. I crave it so much that I developed this sauce, which allows me to pour it over anything I want. I especially love it on burgers.

MAKES 1¼ CUPS

1½ cups crumbled feta

2 tsp lemon zest

1 tsp salt

1 tsp garlic powder

¾ tsp onion powder

¼ tsp black pepper

1 tsp dried oregano

½ cup plain yogurt

½ cup sour cream

3 Tbsp fresh lemon juice

¼ cup chopped dill

Combine all ingredients, except dill, in a bowl and use an immersion blender to blend to your desired consistency. Fold in dill. This dressing can be stored in the fridge for up to 4 days.

Bacon Jam

Mango Sour

Sriracha Honey and Herbs

Green Chutney

Tamarind-Date Chutney

Smoked Raita

Roasted Red Pepper Chimichurri

CHUTNEYS & CONDIMENTS

BACON JAM

There is something very special about the taste of smoky bacon and sweet onions together. And believe it or not, what takes this perfect pairing to the next level is the espresso. Enjoy this jam on toast, burgers and grilled cheese sandwiches, on charcuterie boards or even coated on vegetables.

MAKES 2 CUPS

1 lb bacon

2 Tbsp butter

4 sweet onions, thinly sliced

2 tsp salt

1 tsp black pepper

3–4 cloves garlic, finely chopped

3 sprigs thyme, leaves only

2 Tbsp brown sugar

3 Tbsp brewed espresso

3 Tbsp apple cider vinegar

Preheat oven to 400°F. Line a baking sheet with parchment paper. Position bacon strips on the sheet, being sure to not overlap any pieces. Bake for 10 minutes, then flip bacon and bake for another 3–5 minutes, until crispy. Remove from oven and set aside to cool, then chop into bits.

Melt butter in a large heavy-bottomed frying pan over medium heat. Add onions, salt and pepper, then reduce heat to medium-low. Sauté for 25–30 minutes, until onions are golden brown. Add garlic and sauté for 3–4 minutes.

Add the remaining ingredients and cook for another 5–6 minutes. Set aside to cool.

This bacon jam can be stored in an airtight container in the fridge for up to a week.

MANGO SOUR

I serve this classic West Indian condiment with fried bara (page 28), Guyanese Pholourie (page 30), fish cakes (page 90) and other tasty snacks. It can also be added to my Guyanese-Style Cook-Up Rice (page 73) and other Caribbean classics.

MAKES 2 CUPS

4 cloves garlic

2 Wiri Wiri chili peppers (see Note)

2 cups cubed green mango

¾ tsp salt

¼ cup sugar

½ tsp ground turmeric (optional)

1 Tbsp fresh lime juice

1 Tbsp + 1 tsp white vinegar

Combine all ingredients in a saucepan. Add 2 cups water and simmer over medium heat for 15–20 minutes, until mango has softened and flavors are infused.

Transfer to a blender or food processor and pulse until lightly puréed. Mango sour will keep in the fridge for 2 weeks.

> NOTE: Wiri Wiri chili peppers can be substituted with half the amount of Scotch bonnet or habanero chili peppers.

TAMARIND-DATE CHUTNEY

A popular tangy condiment served across South Asia with chaats, samosas and other finger foods.

MAKES 2 CUPS

1 cup pitted dates
1¼ cups tamarind sauce
¾ cup brown sugar
1 tsp salt
1 tsp red chili powder
½ tsp garlic powder
¼ tsp onion powder
½ tsp ground coriander
½ tsp ground cumin

Combine dates and 1 cup water in a saucepan and simmer for 10–15 minutes, until soft. Add remaining ingredients and simmer for another 5 minutes. Remove from heat and use an immersion blender to blend.

This chutney can be stored in an airtight container in the fridge for a week.

GREEN CHUTNEY

A refreshing, tangy and spicy condiment with a plethora of uses.

MAKES 1 CUP

3 Thai green chili peppers
2 cloves garlic
1 (1-inch) piece ginger
2 cups packed cilantro
1 cup packed mint leaves
¾ tsp roasted cumin powder
1 tsp salt
1½ tsp chaat masala
2 tsp honey
½ cup plain yogurt
2 Tbsp fresh lemon juice

Combine all ingredients in a blender. Add ¼ cup water and blend until smooth.

This chutney can be stored in an airtight container in the fridge for up to a week.

SMOKED RAITA

Think of this as a well-seasoned yogurt dip, perfect alongside grilled meats and crudités or as a dip for nearly anything!

MAKES 1¾ CUPS

½ cup seeded and grated cucumber

¾ tsp garam masala

1–2 Thai green chili peppers, to taste, finely chopped

2 Tbsp finely chopped red onion

2 Tbsp finely chopped cilantro

2 Tbsp finely chopped mint

½ tsp garlic powder

¼ tsp onion powder

1 tsp salt

¼ tsp black pepper

1 tsp lemon zest

1 cup plain yogurt

2 tsp fresh lemon juice

1 tsp liquid smoke

1 tsp honey

Gently squeeze out some of the moisture from the cucumber and discard (I drink it).

Combine all ingredients in a bowl and mix well.

This smoked raita can be stored in an airtight container in the fridge for a week.

SRIRACHA HONEY AND HERBS

Pair this delicious condiment with eggs, pizza or wings—it's unbelievably tasty with grilled meats and other BBQ dishes.

MAKES JUST UNDER 1 CUP

2 tsp finely chopped garlic

2 Tbsp finely chopped chives

¾ tsp garlic powder

¾ tsp onion powder

½ tsp dried thyme

½ tsp dried parsley

½ tsp dried dill

⅓ cup honey

⅓ cup Sriracha

1 tsp apple cider vinegar

1½ tsp white vinegar

Combine all ingredients in a bowl and mix well.

This condiment can be stored in the fridge for up to 10 days.

CHIMICHURRI

This vibrant and refreshing Argentinian condiment will breathe life into most main courses.

MAKES 1 CUP

3–4 cloves garlic, finely chopped

1 cup finely chopped parsley leaves

2 Tbsp finely chopped red onion

1 tsp red chili flakes

1 tsp dried oregano

¾ tsp salt

½ tsp black pepper

½ cup olive oil

3 Tbsp red wine vinegar

Combine all ingredients in a bowl and mix well.

Best consumed ASAP, but leftover sauce can be stored in the fridge for up to 2 weeks.

ROASTED RED PEPPER CHIMICHURRI

This vibrant, visual and versatile sauce will elevate most seafood, meat or veggie dishes. It can also be used as a salad dressing or dipping sauce.

MAKES 3½ CUPS

4 cloves garlic

4 cloves Garlic Confit (page 179)

3 cups roasted red peppers

1½ tsp red chili flakes

1 tsp smoked paprika

¾ tsp ground cumin

¾ tsp dried oregano

1½ tsp salt

½ tsp black pepper

3 Tbsp extra-virgin olive oil

2 Tbsp red wine vinegar

2 Tbsp lemon juice

2 tsp honey

1 cup chopped parsley

Combine all ingredients, except parsley, in a blender and blend until smooth. Add parsley and pulse until the sauce is speckled green.

This sauce can be stored in an airtight container in the fridge for up to 5 days.

FOUNDATIONAL RECIPES

GARLIC CONFIT

Guaranteed to be the best garlic you ever make, sweet and mellow. The oil can be used for any application that would suit having a garlic flavor. I often use it to make my Mayonnaise (page 50).

MAKES 3½ CUPS (INCLUDING OIL)

2 cups garlic cloves
1½ cups grapeseed oil

Combine garlic and oil in a saucepan and heat over medium heat, until it begins to boil. Reduce to the lowest heat setting and gently simmer for 20–25 minutes, until garlic begins to turn lightly golden. Set aside to cool to room temperature in the saucepan.

Transfer garlic confit (in the oil) to an airtight container and store in the fridge for up to 2 weeks.

PANEER

Growing up, few things got me more excited than paneer. Seriously, anytime a curry was made with it, my friends and I always went hunting for the paneer.

MAKES 1 POUND

2 L whole milk
5 Tbsp fresh lemon juice

Pour milk into a large saucepan and bring to a simmer over medium heat. Remove from heat, then add lemon juice and stir once. Set aside for 10 minutes.

Strain the mixture through a cheesecloth, removing as much excess water as possible. Run cold tap water over the block to remove some of the lemon flavor and to cool it down, to allow for easier handling. Press as much liquid out as possible and form into a block. Refrigerate overnight until set.

Paneer can be stored in an airtight container in the fridge for up to 3 days.

METRIC CONVERSION CHART

Volume

IMPERIAL OR U.S. → METRIC

⅛ tsp → 0.5 mL

¼ tsp → 1 mL

½ tsp → 2.5 mL

¾ tsp → 4 mL

1 tsp → 5 mL

1½ tsp → 8 mL

1 Tbsp → 15 mL

1½ Tbsp → 23 mL

2 Tbsp → 30 mL

¼ cup → 60 mL

⅓ cup → 80 mL

½ cup → 125 mL

⅔ cup → 165 mL

¾ cup → 185 mL

1 cup → 250 mL

1¼ cups → 310 mL

1⅓ cups → 330 mL

1½ cups → 375 mL

1⅔ cups → 415 mL

1¾ cups → 435 mL

2 cups → 500 mL

2¼ cups → 560 mL

2⅓ cups → 580 mL

2½ cups → 625 mL

2¾ cups → 690 mL

3 cups → 750 mL

4 cups / 1 quart → 1 L

5 cups → 1.25 L

6 cups → 1.5 L

7 cups → 1.75 L

8 cups → 2 L

12 cups → 3 L

Liquid measures
(for alcohol)

IMPERIAL OR U.S. → METRIC

½ fl oz → 15 mL

1 fl oz → 30 mL

2 fl oz → 60 mL

3 fl oz → 90 mL

4 fl oz → 120 mL

Cans and jars

IMPERIAL OR U.S. → METRIC

6 oz → 170 g

14 oz → 398 mL

19 oz → 540 mL

28 oz → 796 mL

Weight

IMPERIAL OR U.S. → METRIC

½ oz → 15 g

1 oz → 30 g

2 oz → 60 g

3 oz → 85 g

4 oz (¼ lb) → 115 g

5 oz → 140 g

6 oz → 170 g

7 oz → 200 g

8 oz (½ lb) → 225 g

9 oz → 255 g

10 oz → 285 g

11 oz → 310 g

12 oz (¾ lb) → 340 g

13 oz → 370 g

14 oz → 400 g

15 oz → 425 g

16 oz (1 lb) → 450 g

1¼ lbs → 570 g

1½ lbs → 670 g

2 lbs → 900 g

3 lbs → 1.4 kg

4 lbs → 1.8 kg

5 lbs → 2.3 kg

6 lbs → 2.7 kg

Linear

IMPERIAL OR U.S. → METRIC

⅛ inch → 3 mm
¼ inch → 6 mm
½ inch → 12 mm
¾ inch → 2 cm
1 inch → 2.5 cm
1¼ inches → 3 cm
1½ inches → 3.5 cm
1¾ inches → 4.5 cm
2 inches → 5 cm
2½ inches → 6.5 cm
3 inches → 7.5 cm
4 inches → 10 cm
5 inches → 12.5 cm
6 inches → 15 cm
7 inches → 18 cm
10 inches → 25 cm
12 inches (1 foot) → 30 cm
13 inches → 33 cm
16 inches → 41 cm
18 inches → 46 cm
24 inches (2 feet) → 60 cm
28 inches → 70 cm
30 inches → 75 cm
6 feet → 1.8 m

Temperature

(for oven temperatures, see chart below)

IMPERIAL OR U.S. → METRIC

90°F → 32°C
120°F → 49°C
125°F → 52°C
130°F → 54°C
140°F → 60°C
150°F → 66°C
155°F → 68°C
160°F → 71°C
165°F → 74°C
170°F → 77°C
175°F → 80°C
180°F → 82°C
190°F → 88°C
200°F → 93°C
240°F → 116°C
250°F → 121°C
300°F → 149°C
325°F → 163°C
350°F → 177°C
360°F → 182°C
375°F → 191°C

Oven temperature

IMPERIAL OR U.S. → METRIC

200°F → 95°C
250°F → 120°C
275°F → 135°C
300°F → 150°C
325°F → 160°C
350°F → 180°C
375°F → 190°C
400°F → 200°C
425°F → 220°C
450°F → 230°C
500°F → 260°C
550°F → 290°C

Baking Pans

IMPERIAL OR U.S. → METRIC

5- × 9-inch loaf pan → 2 L loaf pan
9- × 13-inch cake pan → 4 L cake pan
11- × 17-inch → 30 × 45 cm
baking sheet baking sheet

ACKNOWLEDGMENTS

Sometimes I ask myself, *how did I get here?* My journey wouldn't be possible without the support of those around me. My extended friends and family have certainly helped me reach my goals.

Mom, many of the family recipes in this cookbook come from the best place in my world: your kitchen. Thank you for your unconditional support. As my career has evolved, and life unfolded, I can only thank you for being the best role model one could ask for. I don't know anyone who cooks as well as you do, and I am indebted to you for my success and resilience.

Thank you to Grandma for always having welcomed me in your kitchen and for your bountiful patience with me as I followed you everywhere. You indoctrinated me into our Guyanese culture; your warmth sparked my passion.

Dad, thank you for instilling the importance of a strong work ethic. The values ingrained in me have helped me overcome difficult hardships.

Thank you to chef Adrian Niman, founder and executive chef of Food Dudes, who took me under his wing when I first began my culinary journey. Your constant guidance and kindness have helped me become the chef I am today.

Also, to TV personality and *Cityline* host Tracy Moore, you've always encouraged me to pursue every goal and achievement. It's a great source of pride to celebrate and promote our West Indies heritage.

I would also like to thank my management team at Quell and everybody involved in bringing this cookbook to life, including editor Michelle Meade, copy editor Pam Robertson, proofreader Breanne MacDonald, indexer Iva Cheung, designer Naomi MacDougall, food stylist Melanie Stuparyk, prop stylist Andrea McCrindle, photographers Suech and Beck, and everyone at Figure 1 Publishing.

Above all, thank you to my brother, Jai, who helped open my eyes up to the world. You always kept me on my toes and taught me everything there was to know about sports, music and food. You introduced me to pho, Hakka, regional Indian, you name it... Foods that I still love to eat and draw inspiration from today. Your electric and contagious smile lit up a room. You are and will always be my guiding light.

Last but certainly not least, thank you Sabrina Babooram for your relentless support with this project.

INDEX